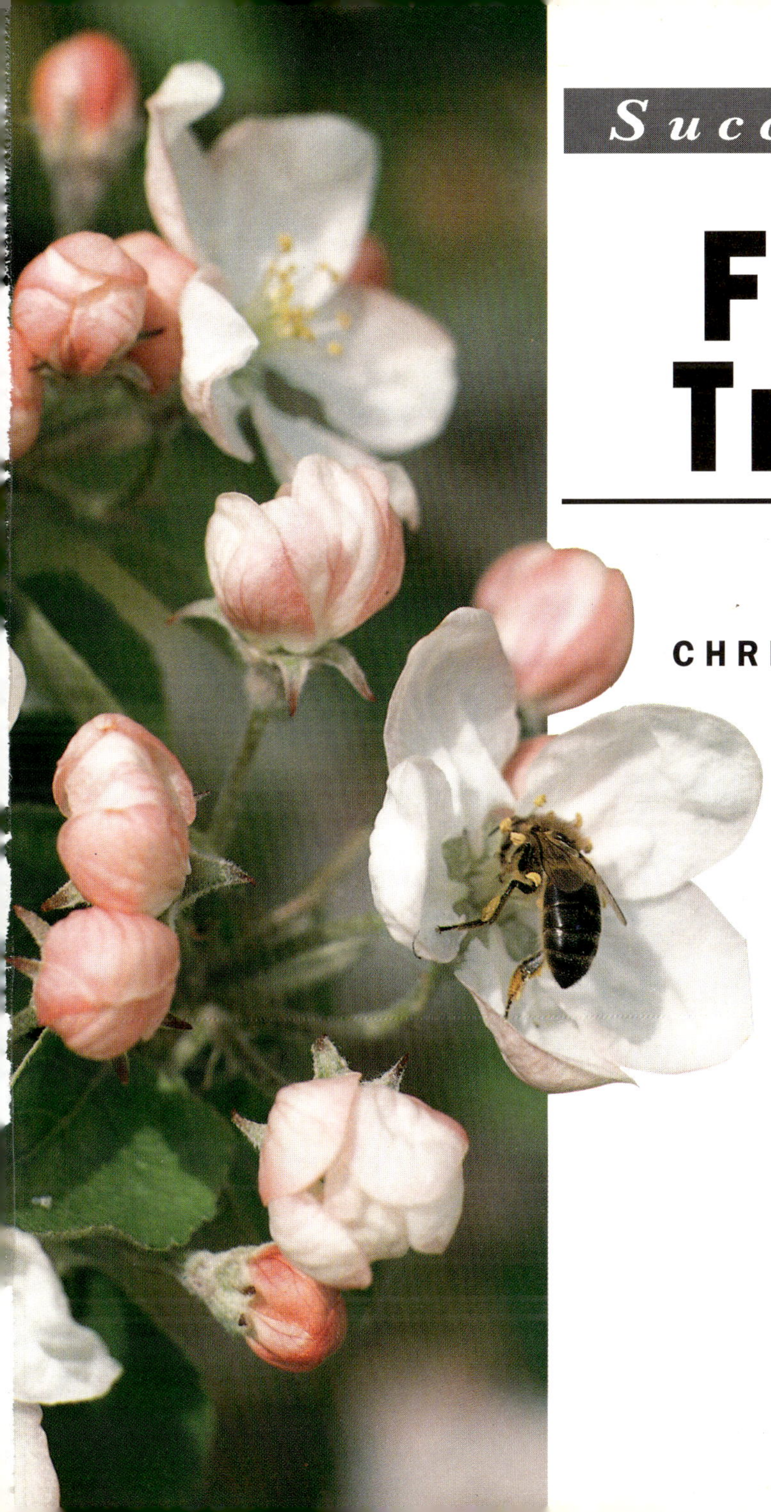

Fruit Trees

CHRISTINE RECHT

Series Editor:
LESLEY YOUNG

Introduction

When you plant fruit trees in a garden you can be sure of springtimes filled with fragile blossom and the buzzing of honeybees and an autumn harvest of mouthwatering fruit. However, you can only really enjoy your home-grown fruit if you know it does not contain the residue from chemical plant protection agents and that is what this guide to fruit growing is all about. In this book Christine Recht explains in a manner that is easy even for complete novices to follow all the important details about growing organic fruit. The most important point of all is your choice of the right tree for the right position, while selecting the most suitable varieties of fruit can prove just as important as being aware of the type of soil that you have and the climatic conditions on site. Excellent colour photographs and detailed instructions on the care of several of the most popular types of fruit will help you to choose wisely. Clear illustrations are used to instruct the reader in the correct way to plant fruit trees, hedges and espaliers. The right way to prune your fruit trees is also demonstrated in simple, step-by-step diagrams. One of the key messages of this volume is the use of organic plant protection which involves using natural remedies in your battle against pests and diseases. Only if you encourage the many useful insects to live in your garden – the organic gardener's first line of defence against pests – will you be able to harvest healthy fruit uncontaminated by chemicals.

Contents

Apricot "de Nancy".

Sweet cherry blossom.

Acid cherry "Schattenmorelle".

The author
Christine Recht writes for many specialist gardening periodicals and is the author of several successful volumes in this series.

NB: Please read the Author's notes on page 62.

Both beautiful and bountiful

All parts of a tree – roots, trunk, branches and foliage – have an important job to do and a sound understanding of these functions will help you considerably in the care of your fruit trees. This knowledge is just as relevant for the giants among the fruit trees as for the smaller trees created by grafting.

It is essential to be aware right from the start that a fruit tree is not always a giant that requires plenty of room. It can just as easily be a small tree that you can pick fruit from without using a ladder. It might even be a bush that begins branching out just above the soil. In principle, all woody plants that bear fruit containing pits or stones can be called "trees" even if they do not quite correspond to the standard image of a tree. A fruit tree in your garden will not only produce nourishing, tasty fruit, it will also prove to be an ornament for the garden at any time of year.

How a tree functions

Once you understand how all of a tree's systems work, you will also understand why certain measures of care are necessary.

The roots

The roots anchor the tree in the soil which is its constant source of nutrients. The roots will continue to grow as long as the tree is alive.

Their delicate tips are covered in fine hair-like roots that are responsible for absorbing water and nutrients from the soil. These tiny roots are continually being produced as the main roots grow outwards and this is why there is no sense in watering a tree near its trunk because the nutrients and water are absorbed by the fine roots under the ground at a point roughly matching the ends of the branches that form the crown of the tree above ground. The old, woody roots serve only as anchors for the tree.

The trunk and the branches

The trunk and branches contain millions upon millions of little channels that transport water and the nutrients dissolved in it from the root system to the crown and back again. The nutrients are thus carried from the roots through the woody parts of the tree towards the leaves. The channels between the bark and the trunk then carry the nutrients formed in the leaves back down

towards the soil. The cambium is situated between the wood and these conducting channels. Every year, the cambium forms fresh wood containing new channels for transporting the precious water from the roots to the leaves and, on its outer edge, the cambium also ensures the formation of new channels for the downwards transportation of nutrients produced by the leaves. This is how the annual "tree rings" are formed so that the branch or trunk gradually becomes thicker. You should always try to ensure that neither the bark nor the cambium is damaged; for example, by tying the tree too tightly to a support stick, through careless handling of a lawn mower, by hammering in nails or allowing deer or rabbits to nibble at the bark.

The leaves

The leaves perform several essential functions. First of all, they are responsible for the evaporation of moisture absorbed by the tree. Only in this way can the nutrients dissolved in the water be properly absorbed. They are then replenished from the soil through the fine

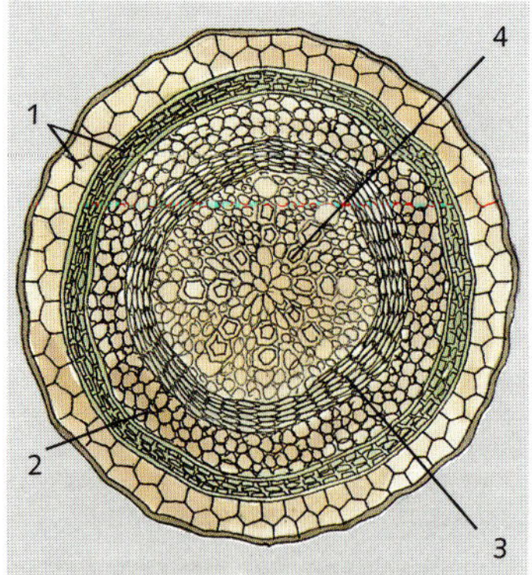

Cross section through a tree
1 bark, 2 conducting channels, 3 cambium, 4 woody part.

How a tree functions
The nutrients and water absorbed from the soil by the roots are transported right up to the leaves. The leaves extract carbon dioxide from the air and, with the help of sunlight and chlorophyll, this is transformed into oxygen and sugars. The sugars nourish the tree, the oxygen is released to the air.

hair roots. Above all, an important chemical reaction takes place in the leaf in a process known as photosynthesis. During this process the leaf transforms carbon dioxide gas into oxygen and sugars with the help of sunlight and water.

The flower
The flower serves to propagate the species after it has been pollinated by insects. From the pollinated flowers fruits are formed which contain seeds to provide the foundation for the growth of a new tree. However, trees grown from the propagated seeds of cultivated fruit trees are unlikely to resemble their parent tree with respect to variety and will often bear small fruit with an inferior flavour. This is because cultivated fruit trees are usually

grafted. In nearly all fruit species, the new flowers are formed during the first month of summer just after the fruit begins to grow. If a tree produces too much fruit, it will hinder the formation of new flowers. This is why fruit trees often carry very little fruit in the year after an abundant harvest.

The right shape of tree for every position
Always choose a stock that will not grow very tall for a small garden, to create a hedge or for a tree destined to live in a large container. Large, standard trees will only have enough room to grow in a real orchard or as a single tree in front of a house. You still have a wide choice as several different shapes of trees are available (see p. 6) within most fruit species. The **dwarf pyramid** shape is most commonly seen in apple and pear trees. The trunk grows up to 70 cm (28 in) tall and the crown remains fairly small. This means that all measures of care and harvesting can be carried out quite easily without the help of a ladder. The yield will be in the region of 10-30 kg (22-66 lb) which is quite sufficient for the average

household. The dwarf pyramid shape is not suitable for a solitary tree in a small garden but several, planted in a row, will form an attractive hedge to create a useful screen from a neighbouring garden. Dwarf pyramids should always be tied to a support post. Apple, pear, peach, cherry, apricot and quince trees can be grown as **bushes** but other types of fruit trees will form crowns that are too large. The stem of a bush will grow to about 60 cm (24 in) high but the crown will spread wider than in the dwarf pyramid shape. This means that the yield will also be higher. Bushes are suitable for solitary trees or as a hedge but only in large gardens. The **low standard** shape is suitable for all types of fruit. It may attain a height of only 1 m (40 in) but the crown will be as large and spreading as that of a tall standard. This form is also easy to harvest by hand but all work carried out underneath the tree, like mowing and care of the soil, becomes difficult as you cannot stand upright underneath the crown of the tree. Short standards are suitable as solitary trees in a small garden; they can also be planted as a hedge if there is enough room.

Shapes of trees
1 bush, 2 pyramid, 3 tall standard are the most important shapes of trees. They are distinguished by their height and the width of their crowns.

The semi-standard, with a height of up to 1.5 m (5 ft), or the ***tall standard*** which has a stem that attains a height of up to 2.5 m (8 ft) is the classic form for fruit trees like apples, pears and plums. The crown may spread out considerably so a tree of this size will require plenty of room. The harvest is measured in tens of kilos. A semi-standard or regular standard may also be used as a feature in an ornamental garden and not just for its splendid blossom. A tall standard can provide shade for a seat in a garden or even be the centrepoint of a larger garden. Semi- and tall standards live much longer than the smaller forms of trees. These larger trees can attain an age of up to 80 years.

The reasons for grafting

A wild tree takes many, many years to grow from seed. Even if you wish to grow your own fruit, you will probably not wish to wait for decades to enjoy the first harvest and you will also want to be sure that the tree will bear the kind of fruit you like. This is why, as a rule, most fruit trees are grafted. In grafting the scion of the desired variety is grafted on to the root (stock) of another strong and fast-growing variety. The grafting point is usually just above the root but in rare cases (cherries and quinces) it may be just beneath the crown. It is visible as a slight thickening of the stem. By choosing a particular stock, both the size and the shape of the tree can be selected as well as its hardiness, suitability for certain soils and the age to which it will grow. It is the root that determines the quantity of nutrients and moisture a tree can absorb. Stocks that do not grow fast will form small root systems, the intake of nutrients will be modest and the tree will not grow as tall or as wide as it might. Stocks of varieties that grow vigorously are used for tall standards. They can absorb lots of nutrients and water and the tree will become a giant. Nowadays, gardens tend to be smaller and there is a greater interest in growing all types of fruit on slow-growing stocks. However, so far this has only been possible with apples and pears.

They can be grown successfully on slow-growing stocks even in small gardens. In the case of plums and cherries, however, so far no satisfactory slow-growing stock that is reliable over longer periods of time has been found. There are also no reliable small-growing forms of apricots or peaches. A walnut tree is always very tall. By nature quinces are bushes, so they are grafted to grow on a taller stem.

Do-it-yourself grafting

When you buy a young tree in a nursery, it will already have been grafted. Many people wonder, however, whether it is worthwhile grafting a tree on to a stock themselves. Generally speaking, probably not. However, certain old varieties of fruit are now coming to the fore again because tree nurserymen and other expert gardeners have recognized that the old varieties are invaluable, not only for their healthy genes but also for their good flavour and resistance to many pests and diseases. To date, though only a very few nurseries have specialised in the grafting of older varieties and this means that it may well be worth a layperson's while to take a scion from a tasty, indigenous apple or pear variety and graft it on to a suitable stock and thus preserve the old variety for posterity. Stocks can be purchased in good tree nurseries. On page 40 you will find out how to graft a scion on to a stock.

The crown sizes of fully grown trees

Apple		**Sweet cherry**	
tall and semi-standard	8-10 m (27-33 ft)	tall and semi-standard	8-10 m (27-33 ft)
bush	4-5 m (13-17 ft)	**Acid cherry**	
dwarf pyramid	2-3 m (7-10 ft)	bush, semi-standard	4-5 m (13-17 ft)
Pear		**Peach**	
tall and semi-standard	6-8 m (20-27 ft)	bush	4-5 m (13-17 ft)
bush	4-5 m (13-17 ft)	**Apricot**	
dwarf pyramid	2-3 m (7-10 ft)	semi-standard	5-6 m (17-20 ft)
Plum		**Quince**	
tall and semi-standard	5-6 m (17-20 ft)	bush	3-5 m (10-17 ft)
Gage		**Walnut**	
tall and semi-standard	4-5 m (13-17 ft)	tall standard	8-15 m (27-50 ft)

A well cared for apple tree in an orchard. The abundant blossom promises a rich harvest of fruit.

Growing your own fruit

Before buying a fruit tree, the following points should be carefully considered: What type of fruit do I like? What type of tree will suit the conditions in my garden? How can I integrate it into my garden? The following chapter will help you to answer these questions and also give useful advice on purchasing.

The right position

Before purchasing any fruit tree you should be clear in your mind about certain important points.
Climate: Not every type of fruit will thrive in every climate. This means that you can choose from among hundreds of apple varieties to find just the right one for a mild, lowland climate or for an altitude of 1,000 m (over 3,300 ft). Whether you have cold or mild winters must be taken into consideration and also the length of the summer season and the average humidity. The best plan is to ask at your local tree nursery which variety of fruit is particularly suitable for the conditions where you live.
My tip: Also ask about local varieties of fruit trees. Many nurseries now include old varieties in their range, which were previously unavailable or forgotten. These older varieties are often extremely tasty and most resistant to pests and diseases. In addition, they are adapted to the climate in which they were first grown long ago.

Mini-climate: The exact same conditions of sun, wind or rain will not prevail everywhere in your garden. The climatic conditions within a limited area are referred to as its mini-climate. Fruit trees grow best in east- and south-facing positions. You can plant an apple tree on the west-facing side of the house, however, as it will prefer moist, cool conditions. Cherry trees prefer a windy position. All other fruit varieties prefer warm, sheltered positions, particularly during blossom time when late frosts can ruin the entire harvest in one night. For this reason you must study the mini-climate in your garden carefully. Frost will often form in low-lying hollows while the temperature on a nearby slope will not drop below freezing.
The soil: The soil conditions should also be checked before you buy a fruit tree as not every type of fruit will cope with every type of soil. To be on the safe side, dig up a sample of soil and have it checked at a soil analysis laboratory. (Ask at your local garden centre or tree nursery

for the address of a laboratory that provides this service. You can also buy a soil analysis kit to use yourself.) If, however, the soil consistency turns out not to be ideal for the fruit you wish to grow, this is no reason to give up. The deciding factor is the right type of stock as the same variety of fruit may be combined with different stocks that grow well on dry, stony, moist or humus-rich soil. Improving the soil may also help, particularly for small-growing species (see p. 42).
Spatial requirements: The number of trees you can accommodate in your garden will, of course, depend on the size of your garden and also on the size of the trees. In principle, solitary trees should always be planted far enough apart so that the crowns will not touch when the trees are mature. If the crowns do begin to become entangled with each other, the fruit will not receive enough light for ripening (see table, p. 6).
Distances to neighbouring properties: A tree whose branches protrude into a neighbour's garden may become a cause of disagreements. For this reason, make sure that you leave plenty of space between the tree and your neighbour's fence. Your legal responsibilities regarding the placing of trees must also be considered and you can obtain advice on this from your local authority. A sensible general rule is that a tree should be planted as far from your neighbour's boundary as you anticipate the diameter of the crown will extend. This will ensure that, later on, no branches will protrude into the neighbour's space.
For example, if the crown of the mature tree is expected to have a diameter of 6 m (20 ft), the tree should be planted at least 3 m (10 ft) from the neighbouring boundary.

In the spring, fruit trees are a delight in any garden or balcony – each flower is more beautiful than the one before.

Designing with fruit trees

Fruit trees can form part of the total design scheme of the garden in many different ways.

A solitary tree can look splendid in the centre of the garden. We recommend choosing a variety that not only bears good fruit but also produces splendid blossom. Such a fruit tree will be just as decorative as an ornamental shrub in your garden. Both tall standards and semi-standards, as well as not too slender dwarf pyramids, are suitable for solitary planting.

A fruit tree hedge may comprise a single row of fruit trees of the same or different species. More artistic hedges can also be grown on an espalier (see p. 19). The dwarf pyramid and bush shapes are both ideal for creating a fruit tree hedge.

The flowers in the photograph:
1 peach blossom
2 apple blossom
3 apricot blossom
4 sweet cherry blossom
5 quince blossom
6 pear blossom

A fruit espalier on a house wall is always recommended whenever you intend to grow fruit species that like warmth. Among these are pears, peaches, apricots and acid cherries. A south- or west-facing wall is the ideal place. Pears, especially, will thrive in such a position, even in harsher climates. Espaliers can be shaped in an informal fashion or in a more strictly formal way (see p. 16). A boring house façade can be turned into an eye-catching feature with an artistically designed espalier. For pears, use a pyramid shape; for acid cherries, peaches and apricots use varieties with broad, spreading crowns.

A proper orchard will probably remain just a romantic dream for most people unless they live in the countryside. Most of the commercial, classic, mixed fruit orchards usually grow fruit for producing wines, cider, etc. on tall standard shapes. The better types of fruit, intended for eating, are often grown as hedges or in rows of dwarf pyramids.

Fruit trees in large containers

Nearly all types of fruit trees can be grown in large containers. However, caring for trees grown in containers is not that easy (see p. 17), the yield is low and the life expectancy of the tree rarely exceeds ten years. None the less, a small flowering apple tree or peach tree in a large container makes a lovely sight, particularly on a balcony in the middle of a city. Generally speaking, all young trees that are grafted on slow-growing stocks can be planted in a large container. Recently, dwarf varieties of apple and peach have been cultivated especially for growing in large

Espalier fruit can even be grown in a large container: here, the apple variety "Elstar" is trained in a double-cordon shape.

containers. Their smaller fruits complement the smaller size of the little standard trees. The dwarf apple "Garden Annie" will grow no taller than 60 cm (2 ft).

Pollination

No tree will bear fruit if it has not been pollinated. Apples, pears, sweet cherries and some plum varieties will definitely require a second tree or, better still, several other trees, for successful pollination. Before buying a fruit tree, it is worth finding out what other fruit trees are already growing in the vicinity as these may fulfil the pollination requirements. If this is not the case, you may have to buy two or three varieties of one species. If you do not have enough room for this, you may be able to graft several differ-

ent varieties on to one tree (see p. 38). Acid cherries, quinces, peaches and apricots are self-pollinating. In the case of the walnut tree, both male and female flowers are produced on the same tree. It is advisable to ask for advice from a good tree nursery about varieties that are good for pollination. There will also be no pollination without bees and other insects so avoid the use of insecticides to combat pests.

Buying a tree

A fruit tree should last for many years, sometimes for decades, so it should not be a haphazard purchase. It can be bought from a garden centre or from a tree nursery, sometimes by mail order. The latter is usually the answer if you want varieties that are not so common. If you are not very familiar with fruit trees, it is a good idea to get expert advice from a local tree nursery. When you buy the tree, it will be one or two years old, which means that you cannot yet tell what it will turn out to look like. The nursery will also be familiar with climatic conditions in the area and should graft on to suitable varieties. Advice should be given while consulting a detailed map of your garden. Only by doing this will the tree nursery expert be able to tell you which stock your tree should be grafted on to, what shape of tree to choose and which variety would be most suitable. From my experience, it seems that laypersons tend to go for a stronger-looking young tree rather than choosing a "skinny-looking" dwarf pyramid shape on slow-growing stock which might be more suitable for his or her garden. Choosing a tree that grows too big will inevitably result in the gardener having to chop it down in a few years' time because it casts shade all over the garden.

The correct way to plant a fruit tree

The planting of a fruit tree is an important occasion. After all, this tree will be part of your life for years to come, so you should try not to make any mistakes when planting it. The tree will spend its entire life in one position, deriving nutrients from the soil and spreading its roots in the ground.

The right moment to plant

A young fruit tree can be planted either in the autumn, that is, at the end of the vegetation period in the first/second month of autumn, or in the spring before the start of new growth, around the first month of spring.

● Autumn planting is better, in principle, as the tree has time to root properly before the winter and will then produce plenty of shoots in the spring. Temperatures may start to become critical during the first month of winter. If the ground should freeze right through, the roots will no longer be able to absorb moisture and the little tree will die.

● Planting in spring is only recommended for species that are sensitive to cold, like peach, apricot or quince. During a very cold winter, these young trees can easily freeze to death.

● Container trees can also be planted in the summer, when they will quickly adapt and start growing.

Immediately after purchasing

After purchasing, young trees should be planted as quickly as possible in the soil, otherwise the roots risk drying out. If you have bought it from a tree nursery or garden centre, the best thing to do is to stand the tree in a bucket of water for several hours. The same goes for a tree that has arrived by mail order.

Do not plant if there is a risk of frost

If frost is forecast, it is better to leave planting the tree until the spring. The following measures should be undertaken to protect it.

● Dig a pit 30 cm (12 in) deep in a sheltered position.

● Stand the tree in the hole with its roots slightly on a slant.

● Cover the roots with the soil that was removed.

● Cover the entire pit with a thick layer of straw.

Checking the soil

If you do not already know what type of soil you have in your garden or what nutrients it contains, then it is time to take a soil sample. It would be better still to have the soil sample analysed before buying your young tree (soil analysis kits can be obtained in the gardening trade).

The planting hole

The planting hole need not be very deep but should have a fairly large diameter. Apart from pears, which drive a tap root deep down into the soil, all other fruit trees produce flat, long roots just beneath the surface of the soil. These roots should be given the chance to spread their soft tips as far as possible. If the soil is very compacted, it might be a good idea to break it up in several places with a pickaxe, otherwise the tree might end up standing in a pool of water. If the fine roots cannot spread unhindered, the entire tree will not be able to grow properly.

Improving the soil

Before the advent of tractors which could be used to remove large tree stumps from the ground, orchard owners used to allow old stumps to burn away slowly and the ash thus supplied fertilizer for the new tree. As a rule, it is sufficient to sprinkle a bucket of woodash and two handfuls of bonemeal on the loosened soil of the planting hole, plus one or two buckets of ripe compost. If the soil analysis results show that the soil is deficient in certain nutrients, these will have to be added (see p. 22). How to plant the tree is shown on pages 14-15.

A support post

All trees should be tied to a support
post after planting.

● For dwarf pyramid fruit trees,
choose a strong post that will last a
long time as the young tree needs
to be tied to it for as long as it lives.
The roots of weaker stocks are so
small and fine that the tree could be
knocked over in strong wind. The
post will have to be replaced after
some years if it has rotted away.

● For semi-standard or tall standard trees, a simple tomato cane
should be sufficient. It can be
removed sometime during the
second year.

Planting on a slope

If you plant your fruit tree on a
slope, the planting hole should be a
little larger and much deeper on the
upperside. In this way, the tree will
end up standing on a flat area within the slope. To prevent heavy rain
from washing the soil away, secure
the front edge of the planting area
with a few large stones or thick
planks.

Planting in a row

If you have planted several pyramid-
shaped bushes in a row, for exmple
as a hedge, it is better not to dig
separate planting holes but,
instead, to dig a 2 m (7 ft) wide
trench and loosen and improve the
soil. This will create a planting bed
that will allow the small trees to
thrive.

My tip: If you are removing old
trees and placing new trees in the
same holes, change the species of
fruit: plant fruit with pips where you
previously grew fruits with stones
and vice versa.

There are many different varieties of plum to suit every type of climate.

Planting

Planting a tree

Before planting, make sure you have the following tools to hand: a spade, hoe, fork, shovel, pickaxe, support post, strong rope or tie and a watering can or garden hose. Make sure that you have given careful thought to the site. How much sunlight will the tree receive during the day? Does the site get frosted in the winter? Will the garden hose reach far enough?

Planting

(illustration 1)

Digging the hole: The hole should be dug to a spade's depth and to the diameter of 1.5 m (5 ft). Place the soil to one side and loosen the soil on the floor of the planting hole to a spade's depth. This is best done with a fork which should be driven into the soil at intervals of 10 cm (4 in). Moving the handle back and forth will loosen the soil. You will need a pickaxe if the soil is compacted. Afterwards, crumble up the soil with a hoe. Add nutrients to this loosened layer: for example, a bucket of woodash and two handfuls of bonemeal with two buckets of ripe compost on top.

NB: If the plant was not pruned ready for planting when it was purchased, carry this procedure out now. Illustrations 3-6 on page 15 will show you how to do this.

Planting: The support post should be hammered into the ground before actually planting the tree (see illustration 2). If you were to do it afterwards you would damage the roots of the young tree. Now stand the tree in the planting hole in such a way that the grafting point is 10-15 cm (4-6 in) above the surface of the ground. Only in the case of quinces or pears grafted on to quinces should the grafting point be level with the ground. Now shovel

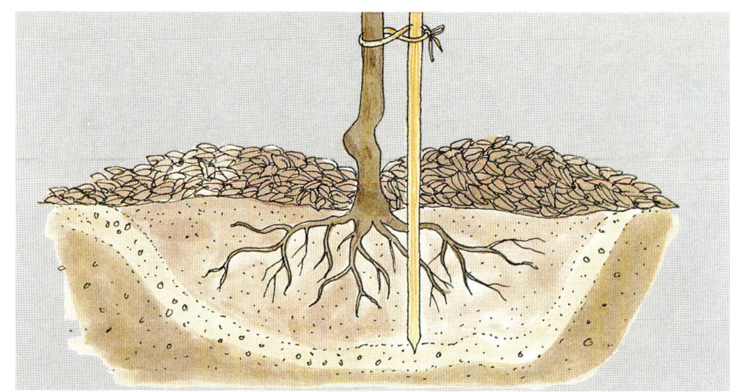

1 *Strew a little wood ash and bonemeal on the floor of the planting pit, then add a bucketful of compost. Fill up with the extracted soil. Mulch around the base of the tree.*

the well-crumbled soil back into the hole. It should be put back in the same sequence as when it was dug out, so that the soil that came out last is the first to go back in. The top layer should go back on top. While doing this, lift the tree up and down slightly several times so that the soil will settle well between the roots. Do not replace a top layer of turf if there was one. The grass would absorb too many nutrients and take water from the tree. Once the tree is planted properly in its

hole, you should check whether it is standing straight. Now carefully tread down the soil and then water well. The soil will settle and you will have to add more. A mulching layer of straw, grass cuttings or bark will protect the tree for the first few months. This will also ensure that the soil remains loose and moist.

Tying the tree to a support post
(illustration 2)

A soft coconut-fibre rope or even an old nylon stocking, if you have nothing else, should be wrapped firmly around the stem and post in a figure of eight. During the first few months, retie the rope often as it should never be allowed to cut into the stem because this would interfere with the flow of sap.

Once the tree is planted you may need to provide protection against damage by dogs digging, cats using it as a scratching post or animals nibbling at the trunk. Wrap sacking or plastic round the young stem.

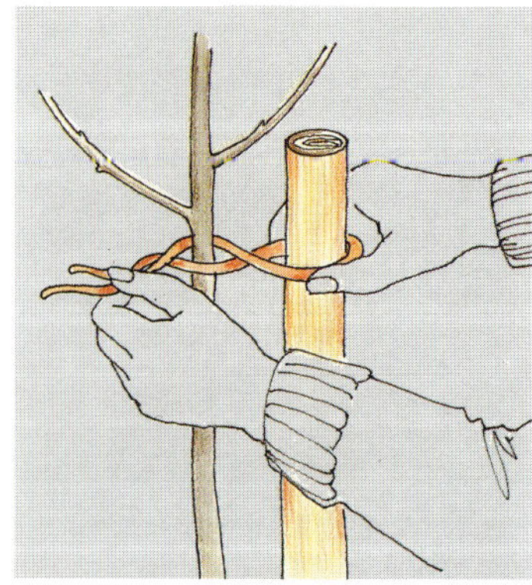

2 *Tie the tree to a support stake with a figure of eight loop.*

The planting cut

Any good tree nursery will carry out a planting cut for you at the time of purchase if you ask. If need be, you can also do this yourself before planting.

Cutting level

(illustration 3)

Before planting, all three main shoots should be cut in such a way that the top buds are on the same level, i.e. on one horizontal line. This will ensure that, during the following year, all new shoots and extensions of the main branches will be of the same length and strength. The central shoot should remain about 20 cm (8 in) longer than the lateral shoots.

The branches

(illustration 4)

An unpruned young tree has several branches: the central branch, the lateral branches and the inferior shoots. The central shoot is easy to identify as it is basically an extension of the main stem. For lateral branches, choose three shoots of about the same thickness, which are situated at an oblique angle to the stem. They should not be all at the same level but distributed along

3 The top buds should all be at the same height; the central leader is 20 cm (8 in) longer.

a 50 cm (20 in) section of the stem. If the lateral shoots are too close together, they may break. All other laterals apart from the main laterals should be cut off close to the stem. You can allow two or three unpruned, weaker branches to remain as they will produce many leaves during the following year and will help to feed the tree through photosynthesis.

Cutting laterals: The three laterals that you have chosen should be shortened by about half for fruit with pips (fruit with stones by about two-thirds). Always cut above a bud that points outwards. This will encourage all buds to shoot in the spring.

Training shoots outwards

(illustrations 5 and 6)

The laterals should grow at an angle of about 45 degrees to the main stem. If this is not their natural angle, use a small wooden stick to push the branch outwards or weight it with a stone on a short piece of string. If the angle is too wide, use soft string to pull the branches closer to the stem.

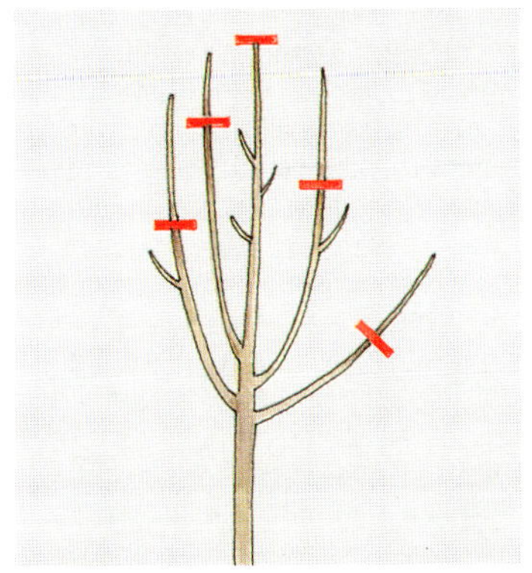

4 Planting cut: shorten the main branch extensions by about a half.

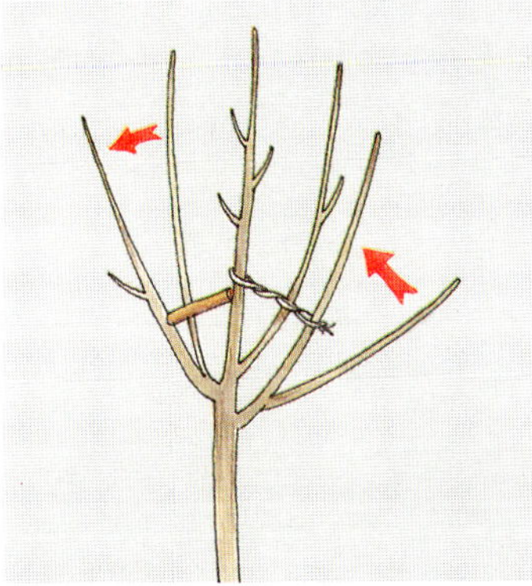

5 Main branches can be pushed apart or tied up.

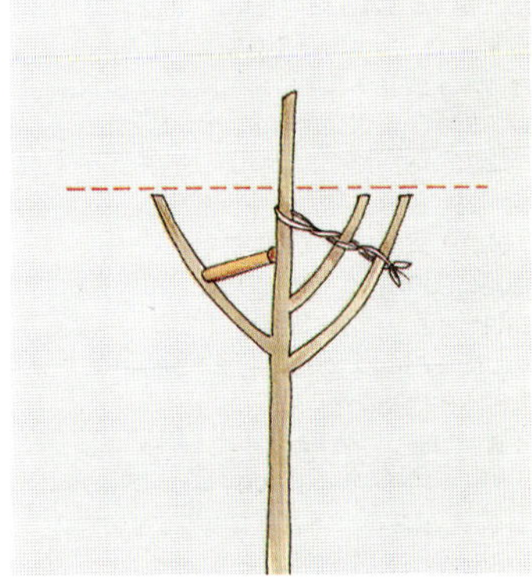

6 This is what a young tree should look like after the planting cut.

Many ways to grow fruit trees

There are many reasons for not just planting solitary fruit trees in your garden: a hedge may take up less space; fruit species that prefer warmth will ripen best on a house wall; a small tree can produce fruit just as easily in a large container on a balcony.

A house espalier

Pear, peach, apricot and acid cherry varieties, which all love warmth, will do particularly well on a warm house wall, on the wall of a garage or against a shed where they will be fairly well sheltered from late frosts, draughts and rain. A well-grown fruit espalier will also provide a house with its own unique character.

NB: Apples are not suitable for an espalier on a house wall as they prefer fresh, cool air all around them.

A grid or trellis is essential for an espalier on a house wall. Unlike ivy or other creepers, fruit trees are not able to hold on to a wall by themselves. They have to be tied on. Build the grid with great care (see p. 18). It will be quite open to view in the winter when the fruit tree has lost its leaves!

The type of tree to choose is one that grows as little as possible. There is a good reason for this as the roots will never be able to spread out properly towards the house wall. Also, the crown of a tree that grows vigorously would not be easy to keep in check.

The planting hole should be prepared in exactly the same way as for a free-standing tree (see p. 14). It should be placed 50-70 cm (20-28 in) away from the foundations of the house. Check the subsoil as, very often, the area around a house is full of builder's rubble in which no tree will thrive. If this is the case, the planting hole should be cleared out completely and filled up with good soil and compost.

Care is almost the same as for a free-standing tree. The area of soil around the base of the tree should be kept free of weeds and other vegetation. An espalier tree will require watering throughout the summer months.

Espalier shapes

There are several different tried and tested shapes for espaliers which are more or less easy to grow even by a novice gardener (see p. 18).

A loose espalier is simple to create and looks good. Pears and peaches in particular are suitable for this shape. Apricots are very difficult to train.

A fan-shaped espalier looks good if trained around a window or balcony. Acid cherry, peach and apricot are all suitable for this style.

The classic espalier shape requires a lot of work and is probably too difficult for a layperson to build. The formal cordon espaliers and palm-shaped espaliers are usually only seen in a few botanical gardens these days. If you really want to grow one of these espaliers against your house (only pears are suitable for these shapes) you should contact a fruit tree expert who is familiar with the art of creating them.

A fruit tree hedge

If you have a small garden and want to harvest different kinds of fruit, it is worth planting a fruit tree hedge.

The shapes of trees to choose are pyramid shapes for fruit with pips and small bushes on slow-growing stocks for fruit with stones. Plums, gages and sweet cherries are not suitable for growing as hedges because of their large crowns, but apples, pears, quinces, acid cherries, apricots and peaches are.

The distances from tree to tree in a hedge should be 2-2.5 m (7-8 ft). If you plant them too close together the fruit will not receive enough sunshine for proper ripening.

Shapes of hedges

The simple tree hedge consists of a row of pyramid-shaped bushes which are placed side by side. Each one has its own support post and will grow as an individual tree. The hedge requires plenty of room.

An espalier hedge is grown against a free-standing espalier made of wires. It will become very dense and the fruit should still ripen well as it will receive plenty of light

A safe place to ripen. The pear variety "Tongern" grown as a house espalier.

from both sides of the hedge.
A Bouché-Thomas hedge consists of trees that have grown into each other and will become extremely dense.

Fruit trees in large containers
Small trees in large containers will not live for very long but they should yield a good harvest.
Suitable for this medium are apples on slow-growing stocks; pears grafted on to quince; peach and apricot grafted on to plum; gages grafted on to blackthorn and acid cherries. Recently, the market has seen the arrival of dwarf varieties specially cultivated for growing in large containers (see p. 11).

Growing your own trees in large containers
Growing your own fruit trees is considerably cheaper than buying ready-grown small trees.
● By a one-year-old grafted tree in the autumn, shorten the roots a little and plant the young tree in a bed in the garden.
● Cut the crown into the desired shape in the spring.
● Pull the lateral branches slightly outward and cut out the shoots that grow inward during the summer.
● During the following spring, plant the tree in a large container.
● For a container, use a suitable compost that should occasionally be fertilized with hoof/horn or bone-meal afterwards.

Further care of a tree in a large container
Fruit trees in large containers should be repotted every two to three years. The roots will have to be shortened on that occasion.
Trees in large containers should be overwintered outside. The container should be well wrapped up in straw and bubble pack or something similar.

Growing an espalier or hedge

Espaliers on house walls

You must take great care when building an espalier grid as it needs to form an attractive feature on its own during the bare winter months.

Building a grid
(illustration 1)
● Battens that have been planed and treated with linseed oil should be dowelled vertically into the façade.
● Place a 1.5 cm (½ in) block of wood as a spacer at each dowelling point to keep the batten from contact with the wall. This will keep the back of the espalier ventilated and the battens will last longer.
● Screw or nail further planed, treated battens at intervals of 50 cm (20 in) horizontally on to the vertical battens.
Another method (suitable for a fan espalier and smaller walls):
● Three or four strong battens dowelled into the wall with spacer blocks.
● Screw horizontal battens to this at 50 cm (20 in) intervals.

How to train the espalier fruit tree
A loose espalier
(illustration 2)
● Tie the two lower laterals of the crown horizontally to the grid, then cut the middle shoot 50 cm (20 in) above it.
● The tree will produce new shoots below the cut. The two strongest laterals should be tied on both sides to the next highest batten, while one is trained up as a central leader.
● Cut off all other shoots.
● During the following spring cut off the new central leader 50 cm (20 in) above the second fork and tie the new lateral shoots to the grid.
● Continue in this way until the wall is covered. Shoots growing upwards from the lateral branches should be tied to the vertical battens and shoots that grow too close together should be cut off. All strong shoots that grow forwards and all those that are not the right shape should also be cut off.

A fan espalier
(illustration 3)
● Bend the middle shoot of a young tree to one side until it is almost horizontal and tie it firmly to the grid.

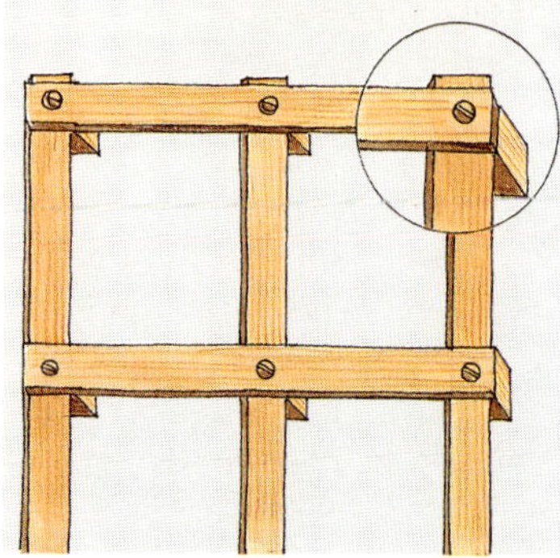

1 A stable trellis made of battens with spacer blocks.

● Strong vertical shoots will grow on this bent shoot and these can then be bent to either left or right and tied to the grid.
● Superfluous shoots can be cut back to the branch.
● Bending laterals in this way can be continued until the entire surface of the wall is covered. The stronger a shoot grows, the more you will have to bend it to train it to the horizontal. When bending shoots, be very careful not to break them. The best time to do it is during the first and second months of summer when the shoots are already strong but still flexible.

2 An open house espalier. This shape can even be trained around a window

3 Fan espalier: the main shoots are growing on the highest parts of the bent central shoots.

Hedge espaliers
The grid
(illustrations 4a and 4b)

a Drive pressure-treated wooden posts (about 10 cm or 4 in in diameter and 2.2 m or 7½ ft long) about 60-70 cm (24-28 in) deep into the ground at 5 m (17 ft) intervals to provide vertical supports.

● Instead of wooden posts, you could also use metal posts that are cemented in. They will last longer.

b Galvanized or plastic-coated wire can be drawn between the posts and pulled tight with a wire stretcher.

● Hammer the two end posts in at a slant and anchor them tightly into the ground with special anchors (available from an ironmongers).

● The lowest wire should be 50 cm (20 in) above the ground; the rest spaced at 50 cm (20 in) intervals above this.

Hedge shapes
The hedge espalier
(illustration 5)

● After planting, train one lateral shoot to the right and one to the left and shorten the middle shoot.

● During the following years, in the first and second months of summer, tie the two strongest lateral branches to the right and left on the wire,

4a *Wooden posts last longer if they are inserted in a concrete holder.*

shorten the middle branch again and cut off all other shoots.

● Once the tree has attained a height at which all jobs can still be carried out without the help of a ladder, bend the middle branch down to the top wire and tie it up.

Maintenance cut: All shoots that grow strongly to the front and back should be cut off and also any shoots that form in the bend of the middle branch. New shoots on lateral branches can be tied up or thinned out. The hedge is allowed to be fairly dense.

4b *Slanting posts are held in position with a screw anchor.*

Bouché-Thomas hedge
(illustration 6)

● Plant young trees at an angle of about 30 degrees. In this form of hedge the grafting point should be close to the ground.

● The strongest shoot will now grow upwards. It should be bent to the other side where it will meet the main branch of the neighbouring tree.

● The shoots should be tied together where they cross. This will form a grid-like hedge that need not be tied up. The roots that grow from the grafting point will give the tree enough stability.

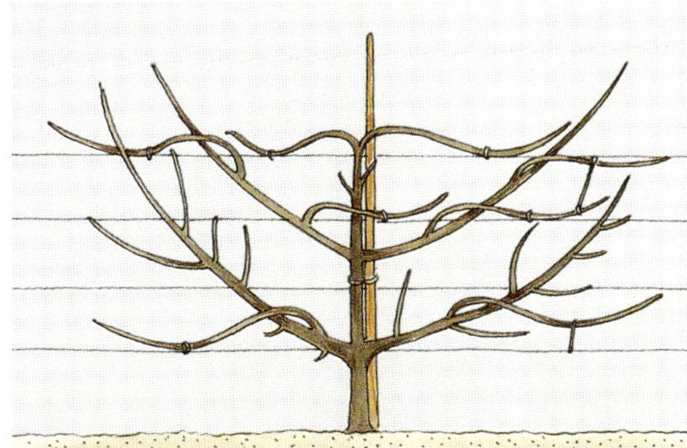

5 *Espalier hedge: The fruit ripens very well as it is receiving light from two sides.*

6 *A Bouché-Thomas hedge supports itself – one tree is supporting the other. It can grow very dense.*

A selection of delicious apples, all of which could be grown in your own garden. In addition to the popular varieties, many older, local varieties of apples are now being offered again by good tree nurseries. It could be well worth your while to make enquiries. Many of the old varieties can also be graft-ed on to a low-growing rootstock.

"Kardinal Bea".

"Ontario".

"Grahams Jubilee" apple.

"Discovery".

"Gloster".

"Gala".

"MacIntosh Roger".

"James Grieve".

"Boskoop".

"Melrose".

"Gewurzluiken".

How to obtain a rich harvest

Only well-cared-for fruit trees will yield a rich harvest. You should make use only of natural fertilizers in your own private garden. This will require some effort but the reward for all your hard work will be very tasty fruit. All other measures of care will depend on the weather, the time of year and the state of the tree.

Proper fertilizing

Fertilizing does not play the greatest part in ensuring the quality of fruit. Far more important is the choice of the right variety, a suitable stock, the weather, pruning and soil conditions. In other words, if you have chosen the wrong variety for your climatic conditions or if your cherry tree is growing in wet soil, the very best fertilizer will not help. You need to fertilize if you wish your fruit tree to develop and thrive for many years and to produce plenty of fruit. The tree is quite capable of absorbing nutrients from the soil through its widely spreading roots over many years but, eventually, all these reserves will be used up.

This is particularly true for all smaller varieties whose root systems are less wide-ranging. The task of the gardener is to make sure that there are always plenty of nutrient reserves available. These reserves are made up out of many components.

Nitrogen (N) is needed by the tree for the formation of new shoots and leaves. Too much nitrogen will result in scab and brown spots in the fruit flesh, the fruit will be watery, acidity will be reduced and the fruit will be tasteless. Too little nitrogen will result in meagre growth and less flower and fruit formation.

Phosphorus (P) is required by the tree for the formation of fruit. A phosphorus deficiency will cause inhibited ripening of fruit and fruit that quickly goes bad. The tree will blossom sparsely and the flowers will look pale.

Potassium (K) ensures that the tree is resistant to pests, diseases and frost. Potassium deficiency leads to fruit that is tasteless and which rots quickly. The leaves will dry up before the autumn. The tissue of the shoots is weakened and very susceptible to disease, particularly if, at the same time, the tree is receiving too much nitrogen. Too much potassium will also have a detrimental effect: the tree will be unable to absorb sufficient calcium and magnesium. The fruit will remain small and sour.

Calcium (Ca) raises the quality of the fruit and is a good soil improver, but the right amount must be given. If there is too much calcium in the soil, the tree will no longer be able to absorb essential nutrients. This means that you should check the pH factor before adding lime to the soil: apples and quinces like a pH value around 6, pears and other fruit with stones prefer values from 6-7. If the pH factor is below this, the soil will require extra lime.

Magnesium (Mg) is a very important nutrient that was underestimated for years. Every plant – even a fruit tree – requires this mineral to produce sufficient chlorophyll which, in turn, is responsible for the absorption of nutrients from the air through photosynthesis.

Trace elements like manganese (Mn), zinc (Zn), iron (Fe), copper (Cu) and boron (B) are absorbed by the tree in minute quantities but they are, nevertheless, vital.

When to fertilize

If you are giving your fruit trees natural fertilizers, give them controlled-release fertilizer which takes a long time to become effective but is also available to the tree for a long time. The exact time at which to fertilize is, therefore, not so important. Even so, it is a good idea to stick to a proper fertilizing schedule for young or small-growing trees so that nutrients are available when they are most needed. Older, tall or standard trees need only be fertilized if they show obvious symptoms of nutrient deficiency. Generally, a layer of compost placed around the tree above the root system will be sufficient.

Fertilizing in the autumn will serve to fortify the young tree and strengthen the shoots in the following spring. Both ripe garden compost and horse manure are equally good.

An orchard near the house. You will have to prune regularly if your trees are growing as close together as shown here.

Fertilizing for flowers should be carried out shortly before blossom time. The tree should receive plenty of water, plant brews or natural liquid fertilizer (see p. 24).

Fertilizer intended to strengthen flowerbuds encourages the formation of buds for the following year. This should be carried out in the first month of summer for pears and cherries, and in the second month of summer for all other types of fruit. This fertilizing can be done with well-rotted compost, manure from stables or with liquid fertilizers to which missing nutrients may be added.

Fertilizing for fruit should be done about four weeks after fertilizing for flowerbuds but, this time, give as little nitrogen as possible. Nitrogen encourages excessive shoot production and the shoots would not be hardy.

What to use

Garden compost is the best fertilizer for fruit trees in a small garden. It should be packed in a 10 cm (4 in) layer on the soil under the tree and covered with straw in autumn.

Manure from stables should be well rotted and spread extremely thinly on the bare soil under the tree.

Organic mixed fertilizer (horn, bone meal or organic-mineral fertilizer) should be worked shallowly into the soil under the tree. It is used on poor soil or soil that is full of clay. This type of fertilizer is also suitable for flowers and flowerbuds. You can prepare your own **liquid fertilizer** for flower production. It is used if fertilizing with compost is not adequate.

Fermented herbal brews, mainly made out of nettles and comfrey, are used in the summer. They should be adequate if the right amount of compost has been given during the autumn.

Wood ash is particularly good for fruit trees as it contains lots of potassium. Tip a shovelful on the soil around the base of the tree two to four times per year (depending on the size of the tree).

"Green" fertilizer, consisting mainly of legumes (for example, lupins, pea foliage, sweet peas) may be used as a substitute for part of the autumn fertilizer. A mass of this foliage can be laid on the soil under the tree as mulch.

How to fertilize

You should not work the soil to any depth underneath a fruit tree as the roots lie close to the surface.

Solid nutrients, in the form of compost, manure from stables, wood ash and organic fertilizers, should only be worked in superficially.

Liquid fertilizers should be applied as follows:

● All round, underneath the far edge of the crown of the tree, use a fork to pierce the soil at intervals of 20 cm (8 in) and move the handle around to loosen the soil.

● Pour liquid fertilizer into the holes produced.

● Then add plenty of water so that the nutrients are thoroughly washed down through the soil.

Further care

A few more tips on care should be observed if you wish to obtain a healthy fruit tree.

The soil around the base of the tree

The circular patch of bare soil around the stem of the tree and stretching to the width of the crown should be kept free of grass or other vegetation as this would draw

water and fertilizer away from the tree. Only in the case of older, tall, standard trees can grass or lawn be allowed to grow over this area.

NB: "Green" fertilizer consisting of legumes or nasturtium is effective against woolly aphid.

Mulching

Place mulch on the soil under the tree. This will keep the soil moist and loose and suppress the growth of weeds. Mulching may consist of grass cuttings, straw and bark. Remove it before autumn fertilizing otherwise mice and other pests will invade the mulch.

Windfalls

Fruit lying on the ground should be collected regularly. If it is allowed to rot underneath the tree it will attract pests and diseases. In particular, the codling moth likes to overwinter in windfall apples.

Watering

Young trees should be watered regularly the first year after planting. Later on, water only espalier fruit trees and trees grafted on to slow-growing stock during very dry periods. Lay a garden hose on the soil underneath the edge of the crown of the tree and allow water to flow gently for about 30 minutes or use a sprinkler.

Injuries

These can occur on the trunk or branches if you have pruned fairly vigorously or if entire branches have broken off (for example, through the action of storms, frost, hail or if the fruit is abundant and very heavy) as well as through nibbling by grazing deer etc. Such wounds are entry points for bacteria and fungi, and also often the cause of the dreaded fruit tree canker. Any wound that is larger than a fifty pence coin should be treated. Use a sharp knife to cut off the edges of the wound cleanly. Cut right down to healthy wood to remove cankers and frost damage wounds. Paint the open cuts with a wound-sealing substance. Very large wounds, for example, created by the breaking off of an entire branch or if wild animals have nibbled off a lot of bark, should be treated as follows:

● Mix two-thirds clay with one-third cow manure (without straw) to make a solid, moist paste.

● Smear a thick layer of the paste on to the wound. Tie a jute sack or some other coarse fabric over the wound. Keep it moist.

Suckers on a pear tree.

A mass of new shoots, the result of injury to the bottom of the stem.

Painting the trunk

Trees that will be standing in full sunlight during the winter months should have their stems painted. The constant alternating temperatures created by frost followed by milder weather will create tension in the bark and cracks and tears will appear that can become a means of entry for germs, fungal spores and pests.

A light-coloured coating will help to prevent such damage. For painting the stem, use a calcium brew which can be bought ready made or a special organic paint for tree trunks.

My tip: If you have only one tree in your garden, you can stand a length of wood against the south- and east-facing sides of the tree during the winter as this will serve the same purpose as a protective coat of paint.

Suckers

These are shoots which sometimes grow up from the base of the tree trunk. Usually, the cause is an injury to the trunk at this point, for example, when mowing grass. The soil should be pushed away all around the trunk but do not dig down and risk damaging the roots. Then cut off these suckers with a sharp knife where they emerge. If you cut them off even a few centimetres above the ground, they will keep coming back and will interfere with the growth of the tree.

Shoots

Vertical shoots may appear en masse after rigorous pruning. They will drain the strength of the tree. They should be cut off flush with the branch during the first month of spring, except for the few that are required for rejuvenating.

Thinning out fruit

This will become necessary if a tree, particularly pear, peach and certain apple varieties, produces too much fruit. Such thinning out can only be carried out on dwarf pyramid shaped trees. In the second month of summer, when the fruit is about the size of a walnut, take out about half the crop. Allow only the largest fruits to remain on the tree and in such a way that they are spaced at approximately 10 cm (4 in) intervals. This results in the remaining fruit growing larger and the bud formation for the following year, which is occuring at this time, will also be better. Never do this until after the first month of summer is over as around this time many fruit trees drop a lot of excess small, green fruit anyway.

Shaping fruit trees

If you allow a fruit tree to grow wild, it will soon display a dense, untidy crown that will produce very few, small fruits and in which fungal diseases will soon spread. As the branches become older and older, only a few weak shoots will be formed. Pruning a fruit tree is absolutely vital for its survival and well-being.

It must be said from the start that you cannot learn how to prune properly from a book. If you have several fruit trees in your garden, you would do well to take an evening course in fruit tree pruning during the winter. Fruit growing societies, gardening clubs and various other groups, such as adult education, provide such courses. You can also always get advice from an expert at the nursery where you bought your trees. If you have only two or three trees, he or she will probably be prepared to prune them once or twice and show you the finer points of pruning.

Why prune?

A properly pruned fruit tree has an open crown in which all fruit is able to ripen properly and will receive enough light and sunshine. This is important for the ripening process and for the flavour of the fruit. In an open crown, wood that is able to bear fruit is formed along the entire branch not just at the tips. This results in a greater yield and about the same amount every year. Properly pruned trees are also known to be more resistant to disease. Fungal diseases, in particular, do not stand a chance as the leaves dry off quickly after a rainfall and never provide the moist, warm micro-climate in the crown that encourages disease. Pruning a tree is, therefore, also a preventive measure for protecting the tree.

Can a tree be pruned at any age?

We have already discussed the planting cut on page 15. This is not enough, however, as a tree has to be cut or pruned in special ways at every age.

A training cut is necessary every year until the crown has attained its final shape and size. Until then you will still need to train branches and tie them up. During this period, main branches that have not yet developed properly can be replaced by new young shoots.

The maintenance cut serves to keep the crown in good shape. Only excess shoots are taken away from then on so that enough fruit-bearing wood can develop.

The rejuvenating cut should begin when no more fruit shoots appear on old wood. In the case of a small-growing tree this may be after ten years, in the case of a tall standard it may be after twenty years. After that, pruning is quite radical.

A thinning out cut becomes necessary for very old, uncared-for fruit trees that have not been pruned for many years and also for fruit species that are not normally given a training cut in the usual way. Here, too, radical cutting will be necessary to ensure that you obtain new fruit-bearing wood.

When to prune

The right time for pruning is late winter or early spring before the sap has started rising again. At this time, when there is no foliage on the tree, it is easy to see where corrective cuts should be carried out.

The summer pruning of young trees is done more often these days than it was in the past. It is carried out in addition to the winter cut and should be done during the second and third months of summer. Pruning in summer encourages growth of the crown, as superfluous shoots which are competing with the main branches can be cut away.

A rich harvest is the reward for the correct care of a fruit tree.

Pruning

Tools: You will need a good pair of secateurs, a branch cutter, a bow saw and a pruning knife.

Glossary of technical terms
(illustration 1)
You will need to know a few technical terms in order to understand pruning properly. (See illustration 1.) Every fruit tree observes the following rules more or less:

● All shoots need as much light as possible so they tend to grow in the direction of most light.

● The bud that is highest will shoot most vigorously so no lateral branch should be longer than the central branch.

● Hardly any fruit-bearing wood grows on branches that grow vertically upwards; more grows on shoots on the long laterals.

● Fewer, but stronger, new shoots appear on severely pruned shoots.

● Branches that have been cut back less form many weaker, but still fruit-bearing, shoots.

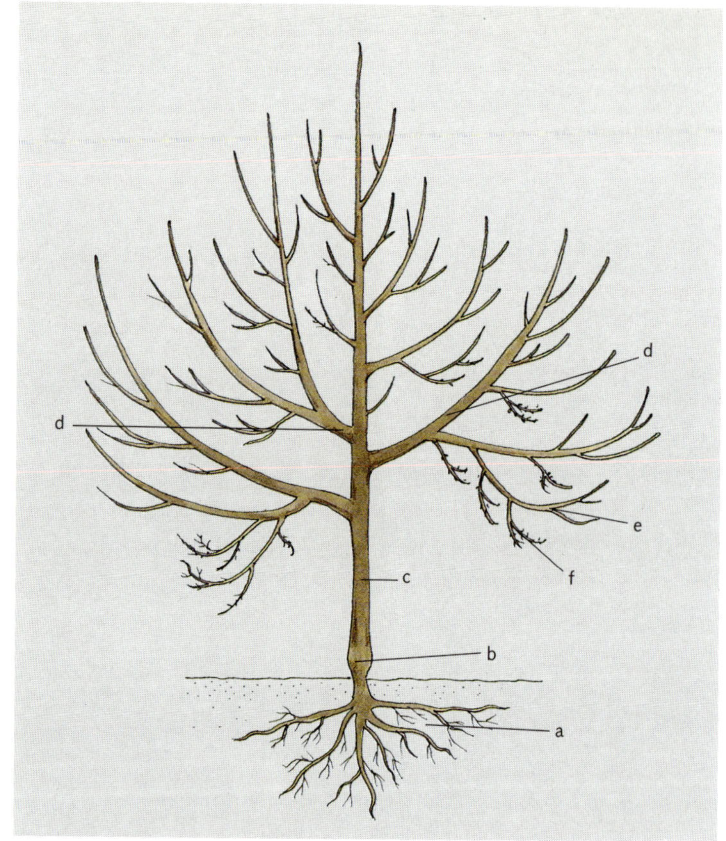

1 The structure of a fruit tree with: a) roots, b) grafting point, c) stem, d) main branches, e) fruit-bearing branches and f) fruit-bearing shoots.

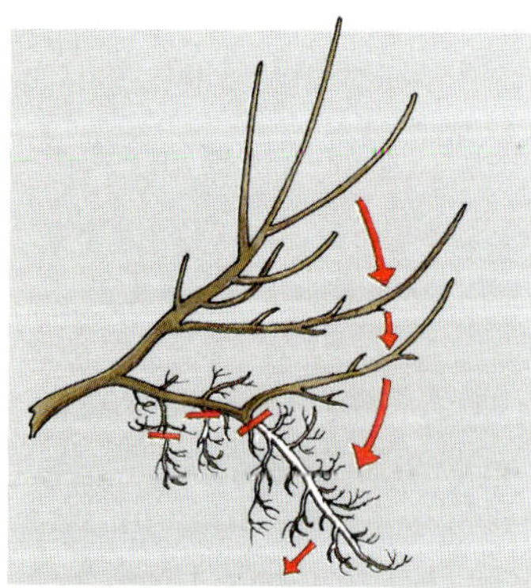

2 Prune the shoots below and new shoots will grow above.

3 Encouraging new shoots. A branch that has been tied horizontally will soon form short, new, fruit-bearing wood.

The formation of fruit-bearing wood

(illustration 2)
Branches that bear fruit over many years tend to hang down low, with the result that new, vigorous shoots appear on the highest point of the hanging branch. Three- to four-year-old fruit-bearing wood which points downwards should, therefore, be cut off at the point where the new shoot appears. This shoot will then bear fruit and, following the natural law, will hang downwards again. This sequence is a continuous process.

Encouraging the formation of shoots through tying

(illustration 3)
The young shoot should be tied horizontally so that it can bear fruit as soon as possible. First, short, fruit-bearing shoots, and then fruit, will appear on the upperside of a shoot. Be careful – if the shoot is tied too low, a vigorous shoot will only appear at the highest point. This means that the angle should be only a little less than 90 degrees. By contrast, illustration 3 shows a shoot that has been cut off, not tied up horizontally. It has not borne any fruit but does show several new young shoots and this can be just as important for training the crown.

Pruning back to the branch

(illustration 4)
All shoots, branches and twigs that are growing too steeply upward should be cut back to the branch. The same goes for shoots that compete with others. The branch or shoot should be cut off with a sharp knife close to the stem so that the cut surface points slightly downwards. This will prevent moisture penetrating the wood and discourage the spread of bacteria.

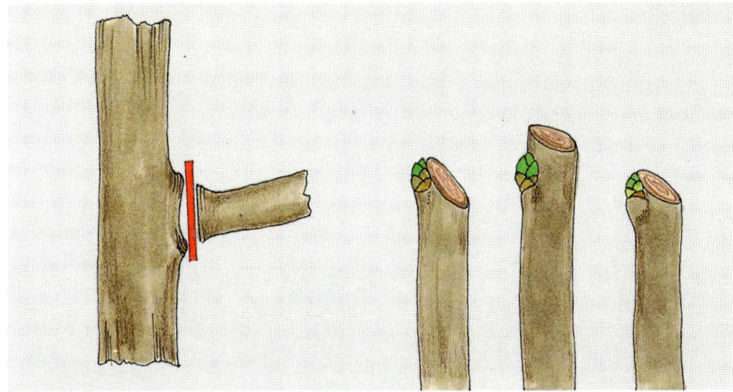

4 Cutting back to the branch. The quickest way for the wound to heal.

5 Cut above a bud. Left – too low, centre – too high, right – correct.

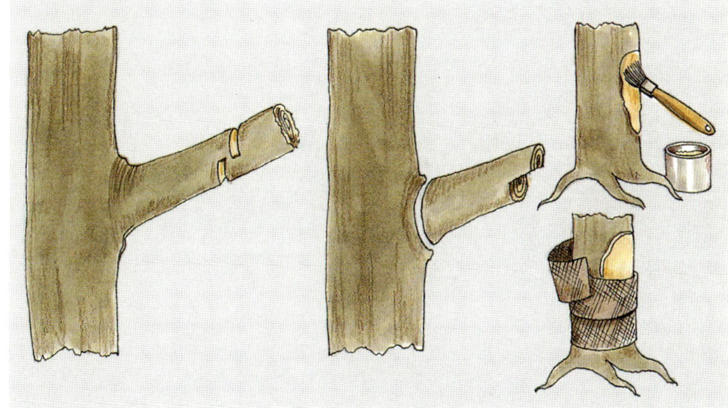

6 A large branch is sawn off in two stages. Right: treating small and large wounds.

Cutting above a bud

(illustration 5)
In order to encourage a shoot to branch out, the shoot should be cut above a bud. This is particularly true for the planting and training cut that is supposed to create a regular-shaped crown. Only if the cut is made correctly above the bud will the shoot branch out properly. The shoot should be cut off 0.5 cm (about ¼ in) above a bud facing outwards.

Cutting a branch

(illustration 6)
Occasionally, a branch will have to be cut off when thinning out and rejuvenating. Saw halfway into the branch from underneath about 20 cm (8 in) from the stem. Then saw into the branch from above, 5 cm (2 in) further from the stem. The branch will break off. Saw off the stump where the branch emerged. A layer of callus will grow over the wound from this point. If you have sawn off a thick branch, the wound will have to be treated (see p. 24).

Pruning

A tree will require different kinds of pruning depending on its age. For all of the pruning measures mentioned below the following advice should be heeded. You must always prune very carefully and sensibly. A fruit tree need not be cut back severely every single winter. Often, small corrections will be quite sufficient. Have a good look at the tree and only prune whenever and wherever it is really necessary!

The training cut
(illustration 1)
After the fairly drastic planting cut (see p. 15), many new shoots will form, not all of which should be left to grow in the crown as it would soon become too dense. The training cut therefore serves to improve the shape of a crown so that it can benefit from light and air and produce plenty of fruit-bearing wood. In the case of small-growing trees, a training cut will be necessary every winter for two to three years, and in the case of tall standard trees, up to eight years. For espaliers it may be necessary to carry out a training cut throughout the entire lifetime of the tree. First, cut out all competing shoots. These are shoots that are in competition with the three main branches and the extension of the stem. Cut them back to the branch from which they emerge. Where new shoots are growing too densely along the main branches, where they grow inwards and wherever too many shoots are growing on the uppersides of branches, they should be cut out at the point where they emerge. Each main branch should be allowed to form a further three branches which fork. This can be done by shortening the central leader and the extensions of the main branches. The following general rule applies. If the

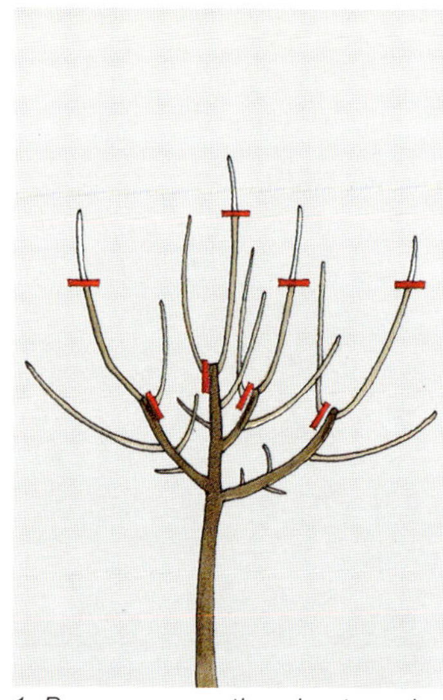

1 Remove competing shoots and shorten extensions of main branches.

new shoots are weak, cut them back radically; if the new shoots are strong, cut back lightly. The more drastically you cut back, the more plentifully the new shoots will grow. Shoots on branches that are not being trained as laterals should be tied horizontally so that they can produce new fruit-bearing shoots. On the central leader, also allow vigorous shoots to remain that are growing at an angle of about 45 degrees. Cut off branches that form an acute angle with the main branch as they will break off under the full weight of fruit. Cutting back the extensions of the main branches and stem is correct if all the buds shoot. Some of these will produce strong woody shoots but many will form fruit-bearing shoots.

The maintenance cut
(illustration 2)
When the crown has attained its proper shape and size, it should look as follows: a stem with a cen-

tral leader and several fruit-bearing branches spaced along it; three strong, main branches, each with three laterals that are spaced at least 60 cm (2 ft) from the stem; several fruit-bearing branches also growing from the lateral branches; short, fruit-bearing wood distributed all over the crown. This wood should be horizontal and keep producing new shoots. If the crown is shaped in this way, maintenance pruning will not be a big job. Every three years, the older fruit-bearing branches, which are beginning to hang down, should be removed so that new shoots can grow in their place. If young shoots have grown too densely on branches or masses of long shoots have formed, these should be thinned out so that sufficient light can penetrate the crown. If a proper maintenance cut has not been carried out regularly, a more drastic pruning will become necessary to thin out the crown.

For the thinning out cut, remove the following branches:
● branches that are growing at acute angles along the central leader
● branches on the upperside of the main branches, which have become too thick (so that new, young shoots can form)
● dried up or diseased branches
● branches that are growing too closely above each other and take light away from each other.
If the thinning out work looks like being very extensive, for example in the case of a tree that has not been cut back for a long time, it would be better to spread the work over two years so that the tree is not encouraged to produce too many new shoots. After this thinning out cut, plenty of long, lanky shoots will grow in any case and these should be cut off during the summer while they are still green (see p. 25).

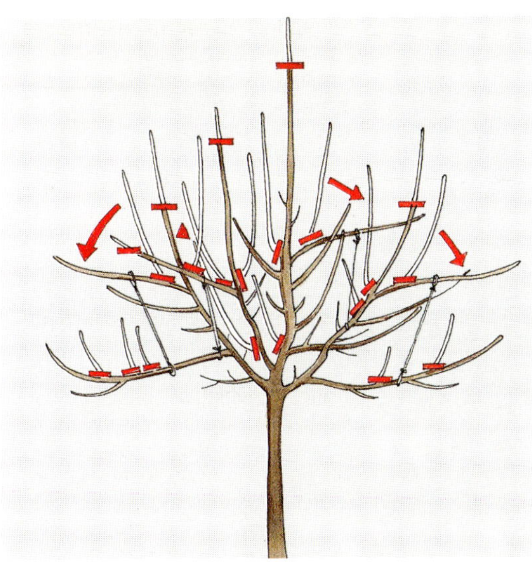

2 *Maintenance cut for thinning out, shortening and always making sure that the crown remains even.*

3 *Rejuvenating cut: a vigorous cutting back of old wood to encourage the formation of new, young shoots.*

The rejuvenating cut
(illustration 3)
When a tree finally becomes old, the yield will decrease noticeably. At this time it will often be well worth rejuvenating the tree. This is a job, however, that is best left to an expert as rather extensive pruning measures will have to be undertaken. The crown will have to be reduced by a third. This means that the central leader and the main branches should be cut back to the old wood. Depending on the size of the tree, this may be up to 3 m (10 ft). Make sure, while doing this, that the shape of the crown remains in balance. At least 50 cm (20 in) of all the lateral shoots growing on both the central leader and the main branches should be cut back to the branch. This will encourage the formation of new tips on the main branches, which will soon produce vigorous new shoots.
None of the lateral branches should be longer than these new tips which means that all lateral branches

should be cut well back into the old wood. The new crown should be opened up. About six to eight branches should remain, well distributed around the stem, and these should be properly pruned.
No shoots should be left growing on the uppersides of branches and everything that looks weak should be taken off the undersides. Fruit-bearing wood should remain. What

4 *Summer cut to keep the crown light and airy.*

is left should, if possible, be horizontal young shoots.
These very radical measures should only be inflicted upon a tree in a year after a poor fruit yield. It will bear a good harvest again during the following years.

The summer cut
(illustration 4)
A summer cut is generally carried out on young trees but it is also a good idea on a dwarf pyramid tree of any age. This means cutting away all superfluous shoots during the second and third months of summer because these shoots will compete with the main branches and the central leader. Also cut away long, lanky shoots that are growing too close together on the uppersides of branches and into the crown. During the summer, vigorous long shoots can be tied into a horizontal position so that they do not turn into main branches but, instead, become fruit-bearing branches.

Nature's own plant protection agents

If you are growing fruit in your own garden, you will obviously set great store by healthy, tasty fruit that should on no account be contaminated with the residue from toxic sprays. Prevention and the use of mechanical and biological plant protection agents will make it possible to do without toxic chemicals.

Biological plant protection means using the advantages and opportunities offered by nature. Your goal should always be to avoid upsetting the natural balance or to risk endangering any living species. Even where the biological equilibrium has already been interfered with, a small garden provides a great opportunity to recreate that natural balance with a little patience and knowledge. Unlike those involved in the mass production of food, you will not need to aim for as large a yield as possible or to produce visually perfect fruit. This attitude is a lot easier in the private sphere. Prevention should always be the first rule before using any pest or disease control measures. During the last few decades, pest control in particular has done more damage than good. Not only were the pests themselves destroyed but, very often, useful insects that were their natural enemies were also wiped out. The fewer useful insects that survived, the more the pests multiplied.

The result was that spraying had to be carried out more and more often. In addition, many pests became resistant to insecticides. A vicious cycle was created that is not easy to break and requires a great deal of patience to rectify.

Prevention through care

Healthy, properly nourished and well-cared-for trees are less susceptible to pests and diseases. The following points should always be observed.

The right position

Every variety of fruit has special requirements with respect to position. Several components play a part in this:
● the climate
● the altitude
● the position with respect to the house
● soil conditions.
Only where all of these preconditions are met can a fruit tree remain robust and healthy. When grown in the wrong position, it will be weak-

ened and thus become susceptible to pests and diseases.
My tip: It is better to abandon the idea of cultivating a particular type of fruit tree if it is not suitable for your garden. This will save you a lot of trouble and disappointment!

The right variety

The choice of the right variety is directly dependent on the position. For example, there are some fruit varieties that will still thrive at altitudes where other varieties could no longer cope. Some fruit varieties are also particularly susceptible to certain diseases or pests.
My tip: Local fruit varieties, of which there are literally thousands among apples and pears, are particularly robust and well adapted to the relevant climate.

The right cut

Pruning a fruit tree is essential but even here one should proceed with care and a clear goal in mind. A tree that has been thinned out properly will hardly ever become infested with fungal diseases as no moist, warm conditions can prevail in the crown. If, however, you cut the tree back too vigorously during one season, this may weaken it and make it susceptible to attack by pests.
My tip: Any radical pruning you intend to carry out is better done in stages over a period of two consecutive years.

The right spacing

In a small garden, the temptation to cram in as many trees as possible is great and they may end up being planted too close together. Trees that stand in a dense group are at risk from the rapid spread of pests and diseases.

These juicy pears of the variety "Tongern" were grown without recourse to chemical plant protection agents.

Avoiding a monoculture

If you plant several apple trees, for example, you should try to choose three or more varieties rather than just one. This will prevent the spread of diseases that are specific to certain varieties and will also ensure better pollination.

Care of the soil under the tree

Young trees require an open area of soil around their base. Grass or lawn would take away too much water and nourishment from the young tree. Small, low-growing trees will require bare soil underneath the crown for their entire lifespan. The soil here should always be mulched so that it remains "alive" and moist. The mulching material will rot in time and provide the soil with nutrients. The root system of a fully grown tall standard, on the other hand, is spread out far enough for the tree to manage without an area of bare soil around the base and therefore a tall standard can grow in an orchard full of grass or on a lawn. You should still avoid digging around the roots, however.

Fertilizing

Fruit trees need fertilizer (see p. 22) but you should hold back on nitrogen. Nitrogen will encourage vigorous growth and large fruits but is not healthy in large quantities as the cells in the fruit tissues are then forced and end up being too soft and therefore susceptible to attack by pests and diseases. It is more important to ensure that the tree has a well-balanced supply of nitrogen, phosphorus and potassium in the right ratios.

Useful insects to combat pests

Useful insects are the gardener's most effective "troops" in the battle against all pests in fruit trees. If the useful insects are encouraged, or even introduced to trees, you can say goodbye to toxic sprays.

Ladybirds are great predators of aphids. Their larvae become active early in the spring. During its twenty-day larval stage, a ladybird can consume up to 400 aphids. The fully grown ladybird is equally as voracious.

Lacewings (Chrysopa vulgaris) are even more useful. Each lacewing larva can eliminate approximately 500 aphids, in addition to small caterpillars and the larvae of other species which suck the sap from leaves, before it enters the crysalis stage after eighteen days. The fully grown insects live almost entirely on nectar which is why they can be coaxed to take up residence by planting many flowering plants in the garden or growing a flower meadow instead of a neatly cut lawn.

Pirate bugs are not beautiful to behold but they are extremely useful. They like to sit along the veins of leaves and at the base of stalks where they are sure to catch their main prey: spider mites.

Predatory mites (Phytoseiulus persimilis) are also specialists in preying on spider mites. Although they are tiny, they are extemely active. If you spray a tree with certain insecticides, such as tar oil winter wash, you will, unfortunately, end up exterminating the predatory mites and not the spider mites!

Hover flies look rather like wasps that have not grown properly but they do not sting. They are important for the pollination of fruit trees and, during their development, the larvae can devour up to 500 aphids each. If you plant plenty of umbelliferous plants between your fruit

Pests that may occur on all types of fruit

Aphids: Crumpled and rolled up leaves, honey dew formation, deformed fruit, masses of green or black larvae. Prevention: encourage useful insects. During the spring, put a sticky band on the trunk. Control: spray with plant soap solution or herbal brews.

Spider mites: The leaves display small, white spots, become brown and drop off. Prevention: the right position; carefully balanced fertilizers; encourage and support useful insects. Control: during blossom time, spray with agents that do not harm useful insects.

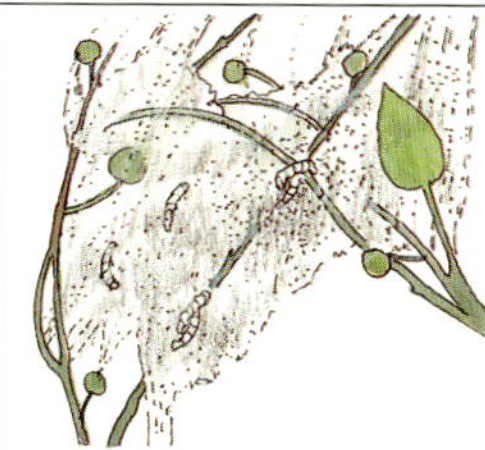

Ermine moth: Masses of tiny caterpillars in white webs in the crown of the tree. Leaves will begin to drop if infestation is severe. Prevention: hardly possible. Control: cut off branches with webs and burn them. Collect by hand in the case of small trees.

Winter moths: Green caterpillars which eat the foliage until the tree is almost bare. Prevention: install a sticky ring in the autumn. Control: biological methods are not possible. The tree will grow new leaf shoots next spring.

Fruit rot: Ring-shaped rotting marks on fruit with fungus formation. Prevention: thin out the crown properly. Collect all fallen rotten fruit, remove rotten fruit from tree during the winter. Control: biological sprays.

Leaf spot diseases: Small spots or holes in the leaves specific to each variety of fruit. Prevention: thin the crown out well, cut off severely infested branches and destroy them; avoid planting in the neighbourhood of juniper as this species encourages the appearance of rust. Control: not possible.

trees, you will encourage hover flies to visit your garden.

Ichneumon flies lay their eggs in living aphids and in the larvae of whiteflies. The emerging larvae will devour their hosts from the inside out. Some ichneumon fly species have specialised in preying on the dreaded ermine moth.

Spiders should be encouraged as they trap many harmful pests in their webs.

Earwigs, on the other hand, have been rather overrated. They are omnivorous and much prefer flowerbuds or fruit to eating aphids. In the spring, they do not emerge from the soil until the aphids have already taken over.

Useful insects to buy

A large number of useful insects can be purchased nowadays but they are intended mainly for commercial operations, large greenhouses and conservatories. Lacewings and *Aphelinus* can be released outside providing the weather is warm enough. They should be attached to infested trees and the larvae will hatch after two days. *Bacillus thuringiensis* is a useful organism that can be used against harmful caterpillars by spraying it on. These organisms are often employed in commercial fruit growing.

Birds

Birds consume several times their own weight in insects annually, so they are extremely important for reducing pests in fruit cultivation. They will only breed where there is plenty of food and that means they will not spend time where insects are being controlled with chemicals.

Encouraging useful insects

The worst enemy of useful insects is people and their endeavours to get rid of pests quickly and thoroughly.

Even some biological sprays will kill off useful insects too. For this reason, a number of points should be observed so that useful insects can continue to live in fruit trees and multiply there.

● Nearly all useful insects overwinter as adult insects in the soil, under the bark of trees, in the casings of buds and other hiding places. Pests, on the other hand, usually overwinter as eggs or larvae. The standard winter spraying, for example with tar oil winter wash, will certainly kill off the useful insects, but only some of the pests as they are protected by their egg cases. If this spraying is discontinued, the useful insects will be present in large numbers at the same time as the pests hatch.

● Nearly all insecticides destroy both pests and useful insects. Pests, however, multiply much faster than useful insects, the reason being that pests live off the fruit trees (and other plants) but useful insects have become specialised to prey only on certain pests. If the pests are exterminated or even severely reduced, the useful insects are doomed to starvation.

● If infestation with pests is severe and you are using agents that do not kill the useful insects, you should ensure that not all pests are eliminated, but only about two thirds. The rest will not cause much damage and the useful insects will continue to find food.

Mechanical plant protection

Other measures can be undertaken to prevent infestation with pests so that spraying may not even be necessary.

Painting the stem or tree trunk

(see p. 24) in winter with a ready made preparation will prevent the pests from establishing themselves in the scaly bark. Painting the bark makes it smooth and it will not then be subject to cracking through the rapid alternation of mild and cold temperatures during the winter. It is a good idea to spray the solution into the bare crown of the tree also.

Sticky rings can be tied around the trunk (also around the support posts) in the autumn to prevent the female winter moth from crawling up the tree to lay her eggs. The caterpillars are quite capable of eating the foliage of an entire tree until it is completely bare. Sticky rings also prevent ants from establishing colonies of aphids in the trees during the spring.

NB: In the case of young trees, the sticky ring will have to be replaced every three to four months, otherwise the ring will cut into the growing stem.

Sticky traps should be wrapped around the stems in the last month of spring. Larvae will collect here and will have to be removed regularly.

Pheromone traps are equipped with female sex hormones to attract the males. The male insects fly up and become stuck. You will be able to obtain these traps in the gardening trade. The traps themselves do not appear to be totally effective but at least they are a means of establishing which pests are attacking your fruit trees.

Fallen fruit should always be gathered up during the autumn. Whatever is not used should be discarded on the compost heap. If you allow the fruit to remain under the tree, it provides ideal overwintering quarters for pests, bacteria and fungus spores. Trees with a very rough, scaly bark should be scrubbed with a hard brush in the autumn to prevent infestation by pests.

Pests and diseases of fruit with pips (apples, pears, quinces)

Scab: Olive green, brown spots on leaves and fruit, the skin of the fruit cracks open and becomes scaly. Prevention: do not grow susceptible varieties; allow enough space between trees; thin out crowns properly. Control: biological sprays from mid-spring.

Mildew: White, powdery film on young leaves and flowerbuds. Prevention: keep the crown open. Control: cut off infested shoots and destroy them; cut out all infested shoots during the winter cut; spray with mare's tail brew.

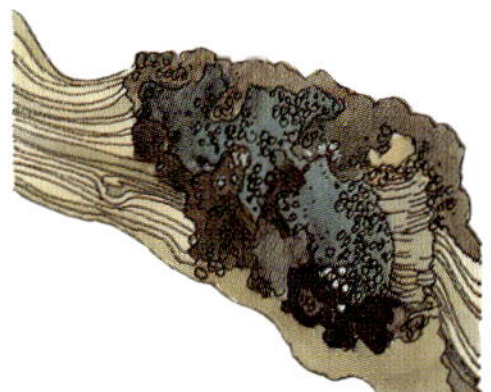

Fruit tree canker: Gnarled growths on the trunk and branches. Prevention: avoid wet, cold positions and overfertilizing with nitrogen; treat wounds immediately. Control: cut out cankers; cover up and seal wounds; disinfect all tools.

Codling moth: "Wormy" fruit, small red worms and tunnels inside the fruit. Prevention: install sticky worm trap rings in the first month of spring; protect useful insects. Control: not necessary.

Brown rot: Soft brown patches on the fruit, underneath which are small brown spots in the fruit flesh; fruit will not keep in storage. Prevention: avoid susceptible varieties; do not fertilize with too much nitrogen; avoid waterlogging. Control: not possible.

Fireblight: Shoots and flowers quickly wither and turn black; very infectious and dangerous. It is a notifiable disease in the UK. Prevention: not possible. Control: cut off infected shoots and destroy them; if necessary, cut down the tree.

What to do in the case of infestation

Even with the best care, pests or diseases may occur on such a scale that action has to be taken if one wishes to avoid losing the entire tree. Here, too, tried and tested methods can be adopted without resorting to toxins.

Mildew and Monilia

At the occurrence of these diseases during the spring, immediately cut off all affected shoots and destroy them (do not put them on the compost heap!). When carrying out a winter cut, make sure that every single affected shoot is removed along with any rotted fruit. Spraying with mare's tail brew is also very effective.

Mare's tail brew: add 1 kg (2¼ lb) freshly cut mare's tail to 10 litres (2¼ gal) water. Bring to the boil, then cool and strain. Spray undiluted as a preventive or if plants are affected.

Biting and sucking insects

If there is an aphid infestation that is so severe that useful insects can no longer cope or if codling moths or other harmful insects threaten to take over, it is time to take action. In this case, a homemade brew may be used to combat the pests.

Nettle brew: Add 1 kg (2¼ lb) of fresh nettle leaves to 10 litres (2 gal) water. Soak for 24 hours and then boil. Allow to cool, strain and dilute in the proportions 1:4 (1 litre or ¼ gal of brew to 4 litres or 1 gal of water) and spray the tree.

Tansy brew: Put 300 g (½ lb) fresh tansy in 10 litres (2¼ gal) water. Allow to boil, then cool and strain. Dilute with double the volume of water for spraying against aphids, ermine moth and codling moth.

Diseases and pests of fruit with stones (cherries, plums and gages, damsons, peaches, apricots)

Monilia on flowers and branches, particularly in cherry trees. Young shoots wither shortly after flowering and die. Prevention: hardly possible, infectious disease. Control: immediately cut off affected shoots and cut up to 20 cm (8 in) into the healthy wood, burn the shoots.

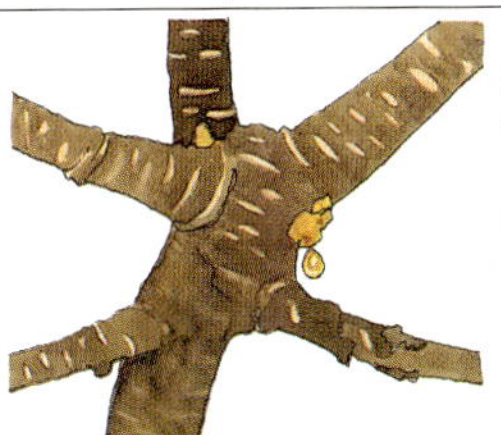

Resin bleeding: Copious secretion of resinous sap on all woody parts; the tree quickly dies. Prevention: not possible, infectious disease. Control: cut off affected shoots, cutting into the healthy wood, and burn the shoots.

Pocket plums: Unnaturally long plums which are flat and brown under a powder-like film. Prevention: keep the crown open. Control: remove affected fruit constantly and destroy.

Peach leaf curl: During the spring this occurs in peach and apricot trees. Blistery leaves that are discoloured whitish-green or reddish and dry up. Prevention: plant robust varieties; varieties with yellow fruit flesh are more susceptible. Control: destroy affected leaves and branches.

Wormy cherries and plums: Wormy fruit. Prevention: early varieties are less susceptible. Control: if infestation is severe spray with biological agents. NB: Avoid this if there are many bees about!

Plum pox virus: Various symptoms, such as severely cracked trunk, rubbery, inedible fruit, light-coloured spots on leaves (does not affect cherries). A viral disease that is notifiable. Prevention: plant varieties that are resistant to it. Control: dig out the trees and burn them.

Soft soap solution: 300 g (½ lb) soft soap or special plant soap dissolved in 10 litres (2¼ gal) hot water. Add a shot of methylated spirits as an adhesive and spray undiluted when cooled to control aphids and scale insects.

Pyrethrum preparations: Pyrethrum is an insecticide that is derived from the flowers of an African chrysanthemum. It works fast against all animal pests but is not entirely safe and should only be used if mechanical and gentle biological methods have failed. Use pyrethrum-containing agents only according to the manufacturer's instructions and note any comments regarding the waiting time between its use and your consumption of the fruit.

Warning: Preparations containing pyrethrum also destroy useful insects! Always wear rubber gloves when handling these preparations. Pyrethrum must not be allowed to enter open wounds as it is a nerve toxin which may enter the bloodstream. Pyrethroids are artificially produced pyrethrum-like plant protection agents that are extremely toxic, very difficult to break down and should never be used in an organic garden.

Organic sprays to buy

Several organic sprays can be bought. They can be used without any qualms but, just as when using chemical agents, the manufacturer's instructions should be closely followed. When using these agents, also check whether they are safe for useful insects, bees and fish.

Warning: Most of the organic plant protection agents are not without their risks either. Children and domestic pets should never come into contact with them.

The best way to grow superior fruit

Young fruit trees are usually grafted in tree nurseries. This is the only way to guarantee that the right variety and shape of tree are obtained. As a rule, grafting is not a technique for the layperson to carry out. However, regrafting new varieties on to a fully grown tree can offer the interested amateur gardener a host of opportunities.

How grafting is done

A fruit tree is grafted by growing a shoot of the desired variety on a chosen stock. Not only does this determine the variety of fruit but a large number of the characteristics of the future fruit tree can also be considerably influenced: its size, the height of the stem or trunk, its hardiness and response to soil types, etc.

The stock consists of the root and a section of stem or trunk measuring about 15 cm (6 in). Stocks are grown in tree nurseries from the seed of specific varieties of fruit through vegetative propagation (shoots, rhizomes, cuttings, etc.). The stocks, which grow first as simple shoots, are cut off about 15 cm (6 in) above the ground during the last month of summer. Depending on the stock, a tree will be tall or short, more or less hardy or have a short or long life expectancy.

The scion is cut from a healthy tree that is known to yield well. Only one-year-old shoots which have short gaps between their buds are used. Scions of fruit trees with stones are cut in the last month of autumn, and those with pips in the second month of winter on the sun-facing side of the tree as the shoots should be fully mature on that side. A 20-25 cm (8-10 in) long piece of shoot with three to five buds is used for grafting. The shoot determines which variety of fruit the tree will bear.

The grafting of a young tree

By grafting (see p. 40), a scion of the desired variety is inserted into the stock. Where the two parts of the new fruit tree grow together, a thickened join is formed at the grafting point. The scion will carry on growing vigorously during the following year and is pruned the year after that, so that it starts to form lateral shoots. Young trees without lateral shoots are one year old, those with several lateral shoots are two-year-old grafted trees.

Grafting on to an adult tree

This measure, also called regrafting, can be carried out by an amateur gardener (see pp. 40/41). It is a possibility to consider if the yield of a particular tree is not satisfactory, if the variety is not suitable for the climate or if several varieties of fruit are wanted from one tree.

Several varieties on one tree

It is entirely possible to graft scions of several different varieties on one tree (this is called a "family tree"). The most interesting situation is one in which a selection of varieties ripen at different times.

Advantages: You will not need another tree for pollinating as the blossom times will overlap. The harvest will extend over a longer period of time, yielding smaller amounts of fruit of different varieties.

Suitable varieties of fruit: In the case of apples, pears, sweet cherries and plums particularly, it is recommended to combine an early, medium early and late variety on one tree.

NB: The shapes of growth should match. Slow-growing varieties grafted with vigorously growing varieties will not grow well. Spindly and drooping varieties side by side will result in an unattractive crown.

Examples: The following apple varieties go well together: "Klarapfel", "James Grieve", "Golden Delicious". With pears: "Frühe von Tróvoux", "Gute Luise", "Tongern". With sweet cherry: "Frühe Meckenheimer", "Spitze Braune", "Schauenburger".

My tip: Plums and gages can be grafted on to one tree.

Two varieties of apple on one tree.

Grafting

Whether you are grafting on to a young tree or on to an old one, you should practise the technique beforehand with a branch you have cut off, as a little skill is required to make the right cut.

Grafting a young tree
The grafting point
(illustration 1)

Every fruit tree that has been grafted in a tree nursery will have a grafting point just above the root. This should always sit above the soil, otherwise suckers will grow here that are difficult to remove. Where trunk-forming stocks are being used, for example, if a quince is required to obtain a tall stem through grafting it on to a hawthorn, you will find another grafting point just below the crown, which may become quite thick in old age.

Whip and tongue grafting
(illustration 2)

The best time for grafting a young tree is during the last month of spring. This is how a scion is grafted on to a stock in the tree nursery. The stock and the scion should have the same thickness, i.e. the same diameter.

● The stem of the stock should be cut diagonally with a sharp knife so that the cut surface is about 5 cm (2 in) long. A tongue should be cut out in the centre of the sloping surface.

● The scion should be cut diagonally to the same length and also equipped with a tongue.

● When joining the two parts, the two cut surfaces are pushed together so that the lowest bud of the scion is opposite the cut surface. The tongues should fit together.

NB: The cambium layer, the layer between bark and wood of both surfaces, should meet perfectly. This is vital if the two parts are to grow together. The tongues help the two parts to stay together and prevent them from slipping. The stock and the scion are tied together with a soft rubber band or raffia. Afterwards, coat the grafting join with tree wax. After six to eight weeks, the raffia should be removed so that it cannot cut into the wood.

Regrafting on to an adult tree

This is the name given to a procedure in which a young scion is grafted on to an adult tree.

1 A one-year-old tree after grafting.

2 Whip and tongue graft. The scion is set on to the rootstock.

In this case, the grafting head of the stock will always be a lot thicker than the scion. Among various different methods of grafting, the two most commonly used ones are as follows.

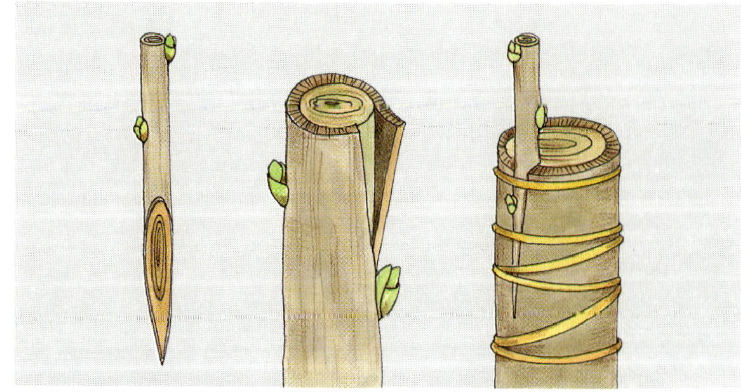

3 Grafting behind the bark. The scion is pushed behind the bark after the latter has been peeled away.

Grafting behind the bark
(illustration 3)

If you want to graft a new variety on to a fully grown tree the usual way is to graft behind the bark. This is a method of joining as much as possible of the cambium of the stock with the cambium of the scion in the best and simplest way. The cambium is the tissue responsible for allowing the two parts to grow together. The right time for this method of grafting is during the spring when the bark of a tree is easiest to loosen. Depending on the regional climatic conditions, this may be any time between the beginning of the second month and the end of the last month of spring.

● The upperpart of the stock should be cut off straight with a sharp knife, taking care that the bark is not damaged.

● From the top edge of the stock, make a vertical cut, 5 cm (2 in) long, through the bark and into the cambium (but not into the wood!).

● Carefully open up the bark on one side of the cut. The scion, which should have been cut diagonally to the same length, should now be slipped under the bark and the bark closed up again around it.

● Tie up the bark and the scion with raffia. The raffia should be wound in the same direction as the bark was laid across the scion. Finally, the entire grafting point should be sealed with tree wax.

Wedge grafting
(illustration 4)

This method of grafting is also suitable for grafting on to older trees. It should be carried out on mild days in the last month of winter or the first month of spring. Cut a wedge, which narrows at the bottom, into the top of the stock. The end of the scion should be cut into the same shape. The scion is then pushed into the wedge-shaped cut in the stock and tied up. The advantage is that wood is placed against wood so the scion sits very firmly on the stock. The only disadvantage is that this method should be practised beforehand as the wedge-shaped end of the scion must fit exactly into the wedge-shaped cut of the stock or the scion will not grow properly.

Care after grafting
(illustration 5)

With both grafting and regrafting, the raffia should be removed about six weeks later so that the thickening of the grafting point is not hindered. Many new shoots usually grow out of the grafting point and they should be cut off as soon as possible to ensure that all the vital strength goes into the growth of the new scion. The scion should always be positioned so that it receives plenty of light.

Pruning

Before grafting on to a fully grown tree, the crown needs some special preparation. The branches that are to be used for the grafting process need to be radically shortened. For fruit with pips this should be done in late winter, and in the case of fruit with stones, shortly before blossom time. The position where the cut was made and where, later on, the scion is grafted on is called the grafting point. It should have a diameter of less than 8 cm (3¼ in). Immediately before grafting, the grafting head should be shortened by another 10 cm (4 in) so that grafting can be undertaken on fresh wood.

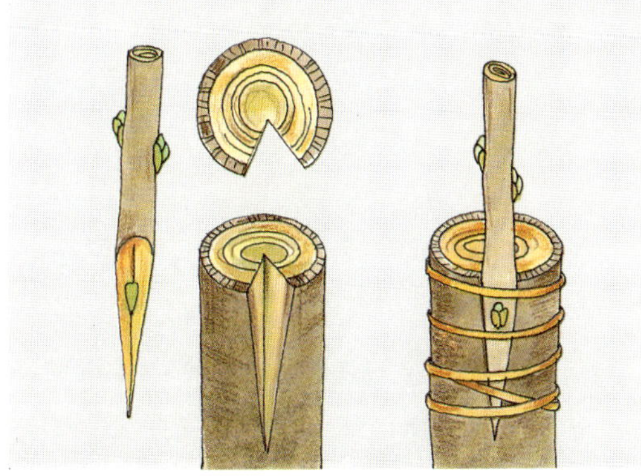

4 Wedge grafting. The properly cut scion is inserted into a wedge-shaped cut on the top of the stock.

5 After grafting, cut off all new shoots around the grafting point (with the exception of those on the scion).

Splendid blossom and healthy fruit

In the spring fruit trees delight us with their wealth of blossom; later on the delicious fruit can be eaten. In order to enjoy fruit gardening to the utmost it is important to know how to care for different species of fruit trees. The following pages give detailed tips on several of the most popular fruit trees. The following descriptions should help you to find the right fruit tree for your garden.

Glossary of keywords

The following pages give detailed instructions for care, with information on:

Name: First the common name, then the botanical one.

Flower: This gives data on the flowering time and appearance of the flower.

Fruit: Notes on the time of harvest and the appearance of the fruit.

Content: Information for people who like to know what they are eating.

Shape of tree: Important tips on the different shapes of trees and the most common stocks used for grafting.

Suitable for: Designs for your garden or balcony.

Position: What you should look out for when choosing the position for the fruit tree.

Soil: In what soil the species of fruit grows best and how the soil can be improved.

Pollination: Indicates whether the fruit tree requires another one for pollination (see p. 39).

Planting: Directions for proper planting.

Maintenance cut: Advice on the correct pruning of the tree.

Fertilizing: Tips on the right medium and suitable quantities.

Care: Tips for tree care all the year round.

Susceptible to: Among these are diseases that the tree is most commonly susceptible to (prevention and treatment, see pp. 32-37).

Varieties: Recommended and popular varieties.

Harvest: How and when to harvest.

Use: Practical tips for the use of fruit.

Storage: The correct way to store different types of fruit.

My tip: Advice and tips resulting from the personal experience of the author.

Abundantly blossoming apple trees in a field of dandelions.

Bud stage ...

... and then, the beautiful apple blossom.

Apple
Malus domestica

Flower: Mid to late spring. The flowerbuds are deep pink; when open, in delicate pink and white clusters. Many late varieties have deeper pink flowers. They appear before the leaves.

Fruit: Harvest depending on the variety, from early spring to mid autumn. Apples come in many different shapes and colours: delicate green, yellow, green with red cheeks or streaks, brownish, dark red. They may be round or elongated, large or small, depending on the variety and condition of the tree.

One distinguishes between eating apples that can be eaten directly from the tree or after lengthy storage in a cellar etc. or cooking apples which are used for preserving or apple juice.

Content: Fructose, vitamins A and C, as well as a few vitamins from the B-spectrum, also, fermentation substances, pectins (important for gelling), calcium, potassium, iron and phosphorus.

Shape of tree: Tall standard trees will not yield fruit until about the age of ten years, semi-standards around seven years. If you purchase four- or five-year-old tall or semi-standard trees, it will be more

expensive, but you will not have to wait so long for a harvest. Pyramid-shaped bushes that are grafted on to the usual stocks can grow up to 2.5 m (8 ft) tall, those grafted on slow-growing stocks will grow less than 1.5 m (5 ft) tall. They are planted when they are two years old, that is, a year after grafting. They will yield fruit for the first time by the second year, that is, at the age of four years.

Suitable for: Tall and semi-standard trees as solitary trees, pyramid-shaped bushes in small gardens, as hedges or espaliers, in large containers. Not suitable for

house wall espaliers as they are sensitive to too much warmth.

Position: Apple trees like to stand in a moist, cool, airy position. West- and east-facing sides of the garden, in very warm regions even on the north-facing side of a house. If planted in a position that is too dry and warm, the trees will remain small and be susceptible to pests and diseases.

Soil: Apple trees have shallow roots but still require a deep, humus-rich soil, preferably loamy. Sandy soils have to be improved as dry soil will cause the apple tree to have deformed growth.

Masses of tempting fruit growing on a well-cared-for apple tree.

Loosen up tough, heavy soil with sand. A pH factor of 5.5-6.5 is ideal.
Pollination: Non-self-pollinating. At least one other apple tree that flowers at the same time will be required in the immediate vicinity – better still, several others that will ensure good pollination. Find out, when purchasing, what the pollination requirements of the desired variety are. Possibly, a third tree will be required as a pollen donor.
Planting: Dig out a flat planting pit, no deeper than the roots of the young tree when spread out. Loosen the soil to a spade's depth at the bottom of the pit. Set the tree at a level that ensures the roots will end up close under the surface of the soil. The grafting point above the neck of the root should end up 10-15 cm (4-6 in) above the ground.
Maintenance cut: Cut off shoots that grow downward and are more than three years old. Vertical shoots and new shoots that grow outward can be left, only new shoots growing towards the inside should be cut back to the branch. Take out long, lanky shoots. The crown should be even and open so that the fruit can obtain plenty of sunshine.
Fertilizing: For young trees and pyramid-shaped bushes, place a 5 cm (2 in) thick layer of garden compost or well-rotted stable manure on the soil under the tree in early spring. If you cannot obtain either, use 100 g/m^2 (about ¼ lb per sq yd) of organic-mineral fertilizer. NB: Do not give the trees too much nitrogen and do not apply lime without having first taken a soil sample. A trace element deficiency may be created if too much lime is supplied. From late spring, if there is a lot of developing fruit, water weekly with fermented plant brews. Older tall, standard trees should only be fertilized if there is visible evidence of nutrient deficiency.
Care: Keep the soil around the base of young trees free of all vegetation; older tall standards may be surrounded by grass or lawn. If the tree produces too much fruit, half of the fruit, particularly small fruit, should be removed from the tree during early summer. The remaining fruit will then become larger and the risk of brown rot becomes less. If there is an overabundance of fruit, the branches will need supporting.
Susceptible to: Scab, mildew, fruit tree canker, brown rot, codling moth, green apple aphid, ermine

"Berlepsch" has a delicate, spicy flavour.

Juicy and crisp: "Schweizer Orangenapfel".

moth, winter moth, woolly aphid, apple sucker.

Varieties: Early: "Beauty of Bath", "Egremont Russet", "Stark Earliest", "Akane", "Discovery".

Summer apples:
"Charles Ross", "Spartan", "James Grieve", "King of Pippins", "Cox's Orange Pippin", "Jonathan", "Elstar", "Jamba", "Worcester Pearmain", "Gala".

Late: "Berlepsch", "Gloster", "Golden Delicious", "Laxton's Superb", "Ontario", "Melrose", "Pomme Cloche", "Granny Smith".

Harvest: Summer apples and very early varieties should not be harvested until they are fully ripe which means that their pips should be brown. Late varieties, apples for storing, should be picked before they are entirely ripe as they will keep better. Do not pick all the fruit at once but pick the ripe ones regularly. Grasp the entire apple with your hand when picking. If you use fingers only, you risk making dents that will later rot in storage. Many varieties of apple alternate between a year with a good harvest and one with a reduced yield.

Use: Late varieties for storage or also for drying. Early varieties and summer apples for immediate consumption, for preserving, for flans, pies and tarts, for juice-making and fruit wine. Freeze cooked apples only as raw apples lose their flavour.

Storage: In a cool cellar with a humidity of at least 80%. Stored apples will remain fresh for a long time in polythene bags. Do not store them together with potatoes as the gas ethylene given off during ripening will cause the potatoes to germinate early and shrink.

My tip: Ask for native, older varieties that have been cultivated in tree nurseries on slow-growing stocks. They are particularly robust in the climate in which they were first raised decades ago and will hardly be at risk from diseases and pests. The fruit of these local varieties is also often very tasty.

A semi-standard apple tree in a large garden. Harvesting is easier than with a standard tree but the crop is no less abundant.

"President Drouard".

Pear
Pyrus communis

Flower: Middle to late spring; at risk from frost in altitudes with a harsh climate. Pure white flowers with red, later yellow, anthers, growing in clusters, appear before the leaves.

Fruit: Early varieties are ripe from late summer, the latest in mid autumn. They are elongated or rounded; large or small; green, yellow, brown, with red cheeks or yellow markings.

Content: Vitamin C and A, also some of the B-complex, plenty of fructose; depending on the variety, more or less pectin, potassium, calcium, iron and phosphorus.

Shape of tree: Trees grown from seedlings turn into large tall standard trees with splendid, cone-shaped crowns. Full yield by the eighth to twelfth year. Pyramid-shaped bushes are grafted on to quince and grow up to 2.5 m (8 ft) tall. They yield fruit from their fourth year. Bush-shaped trees grow to 3 m (10 ft) tall, with a crown diameter of 4 m (13 ft).

Suitable for: Tall and semi-standard tree as a garden tree. Pyramid-shaped bushes as a hedge or single row espalier. Warmth-loving varieties as an espalier on a house wall.

Position: Plenty of warmth and sunshine. Late-ripening varieties will only thrive in a mild climate. Trees

Suitable for a house espalier: "Red Williams Christ".

Delicately sharp: "Dr Jules Guyot".

grafted on to quince are not very hardy.

Soil: Tall and semi-standard trees with deep tap roots prefer loamy, nutrient-rich soil without waterlogging in which the roots can reach down to the water table. Trees grafted on to quince with shallow roots require humus-rich soil that need not be very deep.

Pollination: Non-self-pollinating. Requires pollen from a suitable donor variety. Some varieties are bad pollen donors, so it is a good idea to plant three different varieties.

Planting: During mid to late autumn in light soils; in early spring in heavy soils. Dig a planting pit that is at least two spades' deep and loosen it another spade's depth. Make sure the grafting point is above ground if the stock was grown from a seedling, and flush with the soil for quince stocks.

Maintenance cut: Cut off branches that are several years old and grow inward; also one-year-old shoots if the crown is becoming too dense. Regular cutting back only for espaliers.

Fertilizing: Only young trees during early spring, with 100 g/m^2 (about ¼ lb per sq yd) organic-mineral fertilizer, manure or garden compost.

Care: Mulch pyramid-shaped trees if conditions are very dry.

Susceptible to: scab, rust, fireblight, pear leaf midge.

Varieties: Early: "Louise Bonne de Jersey", "Packham's Triumph", "Williams Christ".
Medium: "Beurre Hardy", "Fertility Improved", "Josephine de Malines".
 Late: "Concorde", "Onward", "Winter Nellis", "Gorham", "Doyenne du Commice", "Alexander Lucas", "Gräfin von Paris", "Madame Verté", "Bristol Cross", "Conference".
For a housewall espalier: "Frühe von Trévoux", "Gute Luise", "Williams Christ", "Alexander Lucas", "Gräfin von Paris", "Madame Verté". For pears for fruit wine and cooking (only tall standards) it is worth looking for local varieties.

Harvest: Harvest a few days before they are ripe. Most varieties will otherwise turn mealy. Pears for making fruit wine can be harvested as windfalls.

Use: Sweet pears can be eaten from the tree; pears for fruit wine making are inedible raw but will make a very good liqueur. Some old varieties are particularly suitable for drying.

Storage: Should be consumed within a few days when ripe.

My tip: Do not plant ornamental juniper nearby as it harbours overwintering spores of pear rust.

Ripe in midsummer: "Schneiders Späte Knorpelkirsche".

"Büttners Rote Knorpel".

Sweet cherry
Prunus avium

Flower: Mid spring before the leaves appear. Clusters of snow white flowers on 5 cm (2 in) long stalks.

Fruit: Ripens early to mid summer. Early varieties usually have soft, juicy fruit flesh. The later ripening cherries have firmer flesh. Colours range from light yellow with a red sun-facing side, to red yellow, fire red and dark red.

Content: Fructose, vitamins A and C, phosphorus, potassium, calcium.

Shape of tree: Stem to 8 m (26 ft) tall, diameter of crown up to 10 m (33 ft). The pyramid-shaped bush is still rare but a rather large crown will develop on stocks like "Weiroot" or "Colt" on an approximately 80 cm (27 ft) tall stem.

Suitable for: Solitary tree. Pyramid-shaped or bushy trees as open loose hedges.

Position: A position in full sunshine. Risk of frost damage in high altitudes.

Soil: Deep, loose, lime rich (pH factor 6-8).

Pollination: Non-self-pollinating. Requires another cherry tree that also needs to be of the right variety.

Planting: From mid autumn to early spring in a planting hole prepared with humus. Grafting point about 15 cm (6 in) above the soil.

Content: Vigorously cut back fruit-bearing shoots after the harvest to obtain a small crown.

Fertilizing: During late winter, 100-150 g/m² (¼ – ⅓ lb per sq yd) of organic-mineral fertilizor or, during the autumn, well-rotted manure on the soil around the base. Enrich garden compost with lime.

Care: Plant nasturtiums under the tree to combat aphids.

Susceptible to: *Monilia,* canker, leaf spot, silver leaf, honey fungus, shot hole, winter moth.

Varieties: Early: "Early Rivers", "Noir de Guben", "Charmes", "Merton Glory".

Medium-early to late: "Compact Stella", "May Duke", "Van", "Napoleon Bigarreau", "Grosse Schwarze", "Sam", "Starking Hardy Giant".

Harvest: Pick for eating raw, for preserving and making juice – shake from the tree on to a cloth.

Use: Preserves, jam, juice, flans, pies, tarts.

Storage: Use within three days.

My tip: To ensure pollination, hang a bucket of water and branches of blossoming wild cherry in your cherry tree.

Acid cherry
Prunus cerasus

Flower: Mid to late spring. Snow white blossom in clusters, minute leaves at the base of flowers. Hardier than sweet cherry.

Fruit: Ripens early to late summer. Light red, dark red to black red fruit with juice which may stain badly. Sharp taste.

Content: See sweet cherry.

Shape of tree: Smaller than sweet cherry. Tall standard, grafted beneath the crown, 1.5-1.8 m (5-6 ft) tall. Bush-shaped trees with a stem height of 70-80 cm (28-32 in), dwarf trees only 50 cm (20 in).

Suitable for: Solitary, hedge, espalier on a housewall, large container.

Position: No great demands on climate. Requires a fully sunny to semi-shady position. Even the well-known "Schattenmorelle" does not like shade, in spite of the German name (*Schatten* = shade) as the name is actually derived from the French word *"château"*.

Soil: Undemanding but no heavy, cold soils with a high water table.

Pollination: Usually self-pollinating.

Planting: A spade's depth, with well-loosened soil at the bottom of the planting pit. Set tall standards as deep as they were in the tree nursery. Allow the grafting point of bush trees to remain several centimetres above the soil.

Maintenance cut: Acid cherries like to form long, whip-like shoots that soon become bare. After harvesting, the fruit-bearing shoots should be cut back to the young shoots that have formed in the crown. Always thin out after the harvest in upright-growing varieties.

Fertilizing: Garden compost or manure on the soil under the tree.

Care: Once the fruit is beginning to turn red, draw protective netting over the crown to prevent birds from eating the fruit.

Susceptible to: Canker, honey fungus, shot hole, silver leaf, cherry leaf roll virus, European rusty mottle virus, little cherry mycloplasma, cherry black fly.

Varieties: "Nabella", "Schattenmorelle", "Morellenfeuer", "Königin Hortense", "Schwäbische Weinweichsel" (tall standard only), "Heimanns Rubinweichsel", "Stevnsbaer".

Harvest: Do not harvest until the fruit is blackish-red, otherwise there will be no proper flavour.

Use: Juice, preserves.

Storage: Use right away.

My tip: If you have no garden, acid cherries will grow well in a large container on a balcony or patio. It will not only yield fruit but also look very decorative.

Particularly popular: "Schattenmorelle".

Plums come in several different varieties.

Plums and damsons
Prunus domestica

Flower: Mid spring. Small, white flowers with yellow anthers on thin stalks in clusters of two or three together. Flowers appear before the leaves.

Fruit: Ripe towards mid summer to mid autumn. The type of plums referred to as damsons are egg-shaped with a pointed end. The dark blue skin has a light bloom on it and the firm fruit flesh is yellowish to orange, the stone flattened. Ordinary plums are larger, with rounded ends and the "seam" of the fruit clearly visible. The thicker skin, depending on the variety, may be dark blue, bluish-violet or deep yellow. There is less bloom than on the damson. The yellow fruit flesh is generally difficult to remove from the roundish stone. The difference between a plum and a damson is not easy to describe. Damsons are mostly used for cooking. Many tree nurseries distinguish plums according to when they ripen (from early summer onwards).

Content: The damson contains vitamins A and C, potassium and plenty of fructose. Plums are sweeter.

Shape of tree: Medium-sized trees with round crowns that can also be grown as flat crowns. These are more practical for harvesting purposes as there are still no varieties with a short stem. Even on slow-growing stocks, they never grow less than 3 m (10 ft) tall. Grafting is carried out either on a vigorously growing stock that is suitable for dry, poor soils or on to the slower-growing "St. Julien" which prefers moist, nutrient-rich soils. Young trees with two-year-old crowns will bear fruit two years after planting.

Suitable for: A solitary tree in a small garden will provide shade for a garden seat, patio or composting station.

Position: Warm, sunny place. The fruit will not be quite as sweet in a shady position.

Soil: Nutrient-rich, humus-rich, moist soils. Some of the older varieties make very few demands at all. However, on no account should the soil be acidic so keep the pH factor at 6.5-7.

Pollination: The main domestic varieties are, as a rule, self-pollinating. Among less common varieties the situation is not quite clear. It is better to make sure that a pollen donor is provided. Blackthorn is suitable for this task if grown as an ornamental bush. In the case of a variety that is

Yellow red "Victoria Plum".

Ready to pick.

known to be non-self-pollinating, one can help matters by grafting a branch of another variety on to the tree.

Planting: Late autumn. Do not make the planting hole deeper than the roots reach.

Maintenance cut: With a regularly yielding tree, only remove bare or hanging branches that are growing too densely together. New young shoots should be cut back by half in order to encourage a rejuvenation of the crown.

Fertilizing: Young trees with organic-mineral fertilizer, garden compost or well-rotted manure in early spring. Only supply nutrients to adult trees if there are definite symptoms of nutrient deficiency (insufficient flowerbuds, chlorosis). Provide lime only after determining the pH factor of the soil.

Care: Both damsons and plums often bear more fruit than they can cope with. In the case of a very heavy yield, the branches will need propping up. Thin out the developing fruit of the yellow "Victoria Plum" after flowering or the plums will remain small and sour.

Susceptible to: Bacterial canker, honey fungus, shot hole, die back, brown rot, sawfly, plum pox virus, plum line pattern virus, necrotic ring spot virus, prune dwarf virus, bark split virus, spider mites, rust, sharka (notifiable).

Varieties: Early: "Ariel", "Farleigh Damson", "Warwickshire Drooper", "Ontario" (yellow), "Ruth Gerstetter" (blue plum), "Magna Glauca".

Medium early to late: "Stanley" (particularly large), "Edwards", "Victoria" "Merryweather", "Pershore Purple", "Marjorie's Seedling".

Harvest: Only pick as many plums as you are able to eat raw. Allow the rest to remain on the tree until the stalk is slightly wrinkled, when they are ripest. Plums are sensitive to pressure and have to be carefully picked.

Use: Damsons are used for cooking. They can be frozen as they come from the tree. In the winter, you can make plum flans with them. Plums are not suitable for freezing but jam, sauce, preserves and juice can be made with both types.

Storage: Use immediately.

My tip: If you love plums but have only a small family, have a plum tree grafted at the tree nursery so that early, medium early and late varieties grow on the same tree. This means you will be able to harvest a constant small supply of plums for three months.

Gages require a really sunny position sheltered from wind.

Gages
Prunus domestica

Most garden centres make no distinction between plums and gages which can both be treated in much the same way.

Flower: During mid spring before the leaves appear. Small, pure white flowers in clusters of two or three.

Fruit: Crop mid to late summer. Some varieties are the size of cherries, yellow in colour and have red dots when fully ripe. Most gages are smaller than plums, round and yellowish-green. Only the "Althans" variety is purple.

Content: Vitamin C and carotin.

Shape of tree: The trees do not grow very large, those with slow-growing rootstocks are only about 3 m (10 ft) tall. Crops appear at about six to eight years of age. As it is best to plant trees with a two-year old crown, you will only need to wait for about four years for the first fruit. The fruit-bearing wood is short and very thin but grows densely.

Suitable for: A solitary tree in a small garden beside a house, beside a patio, also for a large container.

Position: Gages only bear fruit in mild climates. They require a fully sunny position sheltered from the wind. Some of the smaller varieties are a little more robust and some varieties will even ripen in cool altitudes.

Soil: Not very demanding. The soil should be warm, nutrient-rich and not too dry. Sandy soils are ideal as they are warm. However, do ensure that good humus formation takes place.

Pollination: As a rule, the large gages are self-pollinating. Most of the small varieties are not, however. For example, the non-self-pollinating "Graf Althans" gage or the common domestic plum can be a pollen donor for the large gage. "Graf Althans", on the other hand will require a very specific pollinator.

Planting: The best time is in the autumn, in early spring only at cooler altitudes, as the young trees are sensitive to frost. Dig a planting hole to a depth of 50 cm (20 in) and loosen the soil underneath to a spade's depth. Improve light soils with bonemeal and compost. The grafting point should be 10 cm (4 in) above the surface of the soil.

Maintenance cut: Regular thinning out is required to ensure a good crop. Cut out any branches that are too dense or bare. Cut back young shoots by a half. A tree rejuvenated in this way will produce more fruit.

Sweet and juicy "Wilhelmine Späth".

Several gage varieties will ripen at cool altitudes.

Fertilizing: During the first few years, spread 100 g/m² (¼ lb per sq yd) organic-mineral fertilizer or a layer of garden compost on the soil under the tree during early spring. Later, only fertilize when symptoms of deficiency are visible and after soil analysis.

Care: Young trees should always be watered if the weather is very dry. The best way is to lay a garden hose on the soil and allow the water to trickle for about an hour. If the tree is carrying lots of heavy fruit, make sure the weaker branches are given some support or the tree may break. The green fruit can be thinned out in early summer in a tree that has been kept small by regular pruning. This will make the other fruit larger and tastier.

Susceptible to: Scab, bacterial canker, spider mites, and all the other pests and diseases mentioned under plums.

Varieties: "Nancy", "Cambridge Gage", "Early Transparent Gage", "Graf Althans Reneklode", "Oullins Golden Gage" (self-pollinating), "Wilhelmine Späth". As stated earlier, many garden centres or nurseries do not make a distinction between plums and gages, selling them all as plums or possibly also offering a "green-gage". Only specialist fruit tree nurseries will be able to offer the rarer gages and give advice on them. Specialist nurseries do often run a mail-order service which may be of help.

Harvest: Pick gages for preserving when they are not yet quite ripe as the flavour of the preserves or jam will be stronger and slightly more acid. As gages can be harvested in large quantities, the best method is to shake the tree over a large cloth spread out underneath. This makes it easier to pick up the fruit.

Use: For raw consumption, jam, preserves, flans, tarts or the preparation of brandy or liqueur.

Storage: Process gages immediately after picking them as they spoil very quickly.

My tip: Keep a single gage tree in your garden as small as possible or the crop will be too large. Choosing a slow-growing stock is a step in the right direction and rigorous shortening of shoots during the winter will keep the crown small enough.

Peach blossom appears before the leaves.

A peach with red flesh: "Rekord aus Alfter".

Peach
Prunus persica

Flower: Early spring. White to dark pink flowers without stalks that emerge straight from the branches before the leaves.

Fruit: Ripens, depending on the variety, from mid summer to early autumn. Late fruit with yellow flesh is tastier than the early ones with white flesh. Velvet skin.

Content: Plenty of carotin (particularly in the skin) and potassium.

Shape of tree: Tall bush with 80-100 cm (32-40 in) tall stem and open crown.

Suitable for: A solitary tree, wall espalier, large container.

Position: A risk-free crop can only be assured in mild, warm areas. Protect from late frosts as the flowers are very early.

Soil: Very demanding. Humus-rich, loose soil – best with deep gravel. Does not require a high water table. Varieties grafted on to plums will also thrive in heavy clay soil if it is not too cold.

Pollination: Generally self-pollinating.

Planting: Early to mid spring. Loosen the soil and enrich with compost.

Maintenance cut: This produces the largest fruit on "true" fruit-bearing branches, about 50 cm (20 in) long young shoots with two flower buds and one wood bud. Shorten these shoots by a half. This will ensure the production of many fruit-bearing shoots during the following year. "False" shoots (only flowerbuds or only leaf buds) should be shortened to 1 cm (less than ½ in) during flowering. Thin out well after the harvest.

Fertilizing: During early spring about 200 g/m² (less than ½ lb per sq yd) organic-mineral fertilizer. All year round with a layer of mulch, grass cuttings or compost.

Care: Keep the soil around the base free. The layer of mulch should not be allowed to delay the warming up of the soil so loosen up this layer in sunny weather.

Susceptible to: red spider mites, aphids, scale insects, bacterial canker, brown rot, silver leaf, shot hole, peach mildew, honey fungus, peach leaf curl, chlorosis.

Varieties: "Amsden Juno", "South Haven", "Duke of York", "Peregrine", "Rochester", "Hayles Early".

Harvest: Pick with care.

Use: For raw consumption or preserving.

Storage: Fully ripe fruit will keep for about two days, semi-ripe fruit will keep longer but is not as tasty.

Apricot blossom is sensitive to frost.

A "Nancy" apricot.

Apricot
Prunus armeniaca

Flower: Early spring before the leaves appear. The almost stalkless flowers have a red calyx and delicate pink petals. They are very sensitive to frost.

Fruit: Crop from mid summer. The dark yellow, slightly velvety, round fruit is easily removed from the large stone.

Content: Contains a particularly high amount of carotin and potassium.

Shape of tree: Semi-standard, pyramid or small bush.

Suitable for: A solitary tree, best as an espalier on a south-facing wall.

Position: Warm, mild areas. The tree itself is quite hardy but the blossom is easily destroyed by frost. A dry climate prevents fungal disease.

Soil: Loose, nutrient-rich, warm, not too dry.

Pollination: Self-pollinating. It often flowers so early that there are no bees about. An artist's paintbrush may be used to transfer pollen from one flower to another, thus ensuring a good harvest of fruit.

Planting: During mid spring, in loose soil enriched with garden compost.

Maintenance cut: After harvesting, remove inward-growing and spindly old shoots.

Fertilizing: Every spring, before blossoming time, spread 200 g/m² (less than ½ lb per sq yd) organic-mineral fertilizer; in the autumn spread a mulching layer of coarse compost under the tree.

Care: See peach.

Susceptible to: Red spider mites, scale insects, aphids, apricot die-back, rust, silver leaf.

Varieties: "Nancy", "Alfred", "Farmingdale", "New Large Early".

Harvest: Apricots are not sensitive to pressure but if they are picked when they are fully ripe, care should be taken.

Use: For eating raw, preserving and drying.

Storage: Only for a few days. Best fresh.

My tip: Apricots should be protected from rain as they are susceptible to fungal disease. The best place to plant them is against a house wall (south-facing) with overhanging eaves. However, care must then be taken to keep them well watered!

Beautiful quince blossom in late spring.

Pear-shaped "Bereczki" quince.

Quince
Cydonia oblonga

Flower: Late spring. Single, pink or bright red flowers appear on branches that already have leaves.

Fruit: Harvest from mid autumn. Large, yellow, apple- or pear-shaped fruit with a velvety skin and very hard, coarse flesh, appearing particularly at the ends of young shoots.

Content: Tartaric acid, tannic acid, fructose and vitamin C.

Shape of tree: A quince tree grows more like a bush than a tree. It is often grafted on to hawthorn to give it a straighter stem. This type of tree will often grow about 3 m (10 ft) tall, but there are also low-growing bush varieties and pyramid forms. A quince will produce the first proper harvest of fruit two to three years after planting.

Suitable for: A small garden; it looks attractive in an ornamental garden.

Position: Will only develop its full characteristic flavour in regions with a warm climate as the wood is not very hardy. Will require a sheltered, sunny or semi-shady position in a garden.

Soil: Thrives particularly well on light, warm soils with a pH value not over 7. Humus-rich, loamy soil is also suitable.

Pollination: Self-pollinating.

Planting: At the end of the first month of spring in a fairly shallow, well-loosened planting pit. The grafting point should be level with the soil.

Maintenance cut: Thin out only and do not shorten the young shoots as the fruits grow on their ends.

Fertilizing: Well-rotted garden compost or manure containing straw spread on the soil around the stem; other measures are not necessary.

Care: Not necessary.

Susceptible to: Codling moth, apple sawfly, aphids, red spider mites, apple mildew, brown rot.

Varieties: "Vranja", "Champion", "Constantinople", "Portugal", "Von Leskovac".

Harvest: Allow fruits to remain hanging on the tree until shortly before the first frosts.

Use: For jelly, wine, quince preserves. Not for eating raw. Rub velvet off the skin before processing.

Storage: Should be processed as soon as possible or the flesh will turn brown.

My tip: In cool regions, protect the roots with straw mulch during the winter.

Long catkins, tiny flowers.

Walnuts ripening inside green skins.

Walnut
Juglans regia

Flower: During early spring, 10 cm (4 in) long male catkins and inconspicuous female flowers form on the same tree during the appearance of the first leaves.

Fruit: Harvest from the end of the first month of autumn. The kernel is in a hard shell which, in turn, is covered with a tough, green skin. Depending on the variety, the fruit will be large or small, with a thin or thick shell.

Content: Lots of protein and fat.

Shape of tree: Up to 20 m (67 ft) tall; diameter of crown up to 20 m also. The roots extend far beyond the edge of the crown so leave a space of 15 m (50 ft) from all other plants and from the house.

Suitable for: Large gardens.

Position: Sensitive to frost, so only in warm regions.

Soil: Loose, very deep, easy for roots to expand, warm and humus-rich. Very demanding.

Pollination: Self-pollinating.

Planting: Better than a seedling, buy a grafted (expensive) young tree. Dig a deep planting pit, loosen well, and dig right through deeper layers of clay.

Maintenance cut: Should not be pruned. Only remove broken or frost-damaged branches during late summer. Before that, the tree will "bleed" too much.

Fertilizing: Not necessary.

Care: Not necessary.

Susceptible to: Gall mites, honey fungus, late frosts.

Varieties: Recommended walnut varieties include "Excelsior of Taynton", "Leeds Castle", "Northdown Clawnut".

Harvest: Gather up nuts if they have fallen from the tree. By then, the green skins will have dried up and fallen off.

Use: In cake-making, for pickling or eating raw.

Storage: Dry the nuts in the sun for a few days or in a warm place. They should keep until well past Christmas.

My tip: A walnut tree near the house will keep away flies.

Index

The author, publishers and the photographer Friedrich Strauss wish to thank the following for their support:

Niederbayerische Obstversuchsanstalt, Deutenkofen
Institut für Obstbau und Baumschule Fachhochschule, Weihenstephan
Lehrstuhl für Obstbau der TE München/Weihenstephan
Samen Schmitz Baumschule
Fischer, Barnau

Author's notes

This book explains how to grow fruit trees organically. It includes instructions for the use of biological plant protection agents. Some measures of care should be taken when handling these substances: please follow manufacturers' instructions meticulously. Keep children and domestic pets away when you are using these agents. Wear gloves when using agents containing pyrethrum. These substances should not be allowed to enter open wounds (see p. 37). Make sure you store all plant protection agents in such a way that they are inaccessible to children and domestic pets. Large fruit trees often tempt children and even adults to climb them. Serious accidents can then occur due to thin or rotten branches breaking. Always make sure you only harvest fruit using a safe ladder and make sure that children do not climb around in fruit trees.

Cover photographs

Front cover: *Ripe apples.*
Inside front cover: *Apple blossom.*
Page 63: *Peaches.*
Back cover: *Apricot blossom.*

Photographic acknowledgements

Albinger: p. 27; Mein Schöner Garten/Fischer: p. 39, 45, 52, 55 right, inside back cover; Reinhard: p. 54; Scherz: p. 4, 7, 9 top centre, bottom right, 12, 23, 42/43, 59, back cover bottom right; Strauss: all other photos.

This edition published 1996 by Merehurst Limited
Ferry House, 51-57 Lacy Road, Putney, London SW15 1PR

© 1992 Gräfe und Unzer GmbH, Munich

ISBN 1-85391-588-2

Translated by Astrid Mick
Edited by Lesley Young
Design and typesetting by Paul Cooper Design
Printed in Hong Kong by Wing King Tong

Success with
Fuchsias
Series Editor: LESLEY YOUNG

Success with
Your
Garden Pond
Series Editor: LESLEY YOUNG

Success with
Bonsai
Series Editor: LESLEY YOUNG

Success with
Hanging Baskets
& Containers
Series Editor: LESLEY YOUNG

Success with
Roses
Series Editor: LESLEY YOUNG

Success with
Herbs
Series Editor: LESLEY YOUNG

Success with
Orchids
Series Editor: LESLEY YOUNG

Success with
Climbing Plants
Series Editor: LESLEY YOUNG

Success with
Geraniums
and Pelargoniums
Series Editor: LESLEY YOUNG

Success with
Camellias
Series Editor: LESLEY YOUNG

Success with
Cacti
Series Editor: LESLEY YOUNG

Success with
Spring Flowers
Series Editor: LESLEY YOUNG